Information and
Business Performance

A study of information systems and services in
high performing companies

Also available in this series:

Electronic Publishing and Libraries. Planning for the Impact and Growth to 2003
    edited by David J. Brown
Project ELVYN: an Experiment in Electronic Journal Delivery. Facts, Figures and Findings
    edited by Fytton Rowland, Cliff McKnight and Jack Meadows
Networking in the Humanities
    edited by Stephanie Kenna and Seamus Ross
The Value and Impact of Information
    edited by Mary Feeney and Maureen Grieves
National Information Policies and Strategies: An Overview and Bibliographic Survey
    Michael W. Hill
Changing Information Technologies: Research Challenges in the Economics of Information
    edited by Mary Feeney and Maureen Grieves
Innovation in Information: Twenty Years of the British Library Research and Development Department
    Jack Meadows
Teaching Information Skills: A Review of the Research and its Impact on Education
    edited by Rick Rogers
Decision Support Systems and Performance Assessment in Academic Libraries
    Roy Adams, Ian Bloor, Mel Collier,
    Marcus Meldrum and Suzanne Ward
Information Technology and the Research Process
    edited by Mary Feeney and Karen Merry
Information UK 2000
    edited by John Martyn, Peter Vickers and Mary Feeney
Scholarly Communication and Serials Prices
    edited by Karen Brookfield
Scholarship and Technology in the Humanities
    edited by May Katzen
Multimedia Information
    edited by Mary Feeney and Shirley Day

Information and Business Performance

**A study of information systems and services in
high performing companies**

Ian Owens and Tom Wilson
with Angela Abell

**BOWKER
SAUR**

London • Melbourne • Munich • New Jersey

British Library Cataloguing in Publication Data
A catalogue record for this book is available from the British Library.

Library of Congress Cataloging-in-Publication Data
A catalog record for this book is available from the Library of Congress.

Published by Bowker-Saur, a division of Reed Elsevier (UK) Limited
Maypole House, Maypole Road
East Grinstead, West Sussex RH19 1HU, UK
Tel: +44 (0) 1342 330100 Fax: +44 (0) 1342 330191
E-mail: lis@bowker-saur.co.uk
Internet Website: http://www.bowker-saur.co.uk/service/

Bowker-Saur is part of REED REFERENCE PUBLISHING

ISBN 1-85739-108-X

Cover design by John Cole
Desktop published by Mary Feeney, The Data Workshop, Bury St Edmunds
Index compiled by Judy Batchelor
Printed on acid-free paper
Printed and bound in Great Britain by Antony Rowe Ltd, Chippenham, Wiltshire

Contents

Preface

This report deals with the difficult issue of the contribution that information systems and services make to the performance of businesses. The subject is fraught with difficulties, partly because of the confusion of terminology relating to information in the business world, where the term is often associated solely with internally-created information and/or with information technology.

There are also major problems in gaining access and cooperation at a time of widespread economic difficulty and in identifying the exact nature of systems and services when businesses are undergoing almost continuous organizational change, or suffering from various forms of organizational pressure.

In spite of these difficulties, however, and perhaps because the research team began with a coherent model of what they expected to find, cooperation with twelve companies was secured and the results are reported here.

One of the results, of interest to the researchers from a methodological point of view, was the extent to which the original model on interacting factors was challenged and changed through the research process. The main categories of variables were found to be relatively robust, but other factors were also discovered and the general model was enlarged to cover these.

Section 1 presents the research report, while Section 2 gives the results of the twelve case studies in detail. The conclusions of the research team were discussed by an invited group of information professionals at a seminar held at the British Library Research and Development Department in March 1995; a report of this seminar is given in Section 3. The questionnaire and interview schedule are reproduced in the Appendices.

The authors would like to acknowledge the useful discussions held with other members of the Åbo Consortium, and the valuable contribution made by the Project Consultant, Angela Abell of TFPL Ltd. The authors would also like to acknowledge the cooperation of the twelve companies which took part in this study.

Executive Summary

This report set out to investigate the link between effective information systems and business performance. Few investigations have examined this area in any detail. Much of the recent literature has concentrated on the business benefits of the widespread introduction of information technology into the workplace.

For the purposes of this report a theoretical model was tested in high performing companies. In all, twelve high performing companies were included in the sample group. Senior representatives from the companies were interviewed and a questionnaire was administered to other members of staff. A case study was prepared for each company.

The results illustrated the lack of a coherent information policy in many of the companies surveyed. Information professionals have seen their influence diminish, and they have in general been slow to embrace new technology.

The research also highlighted the emphasis placed by many of the companies surveyed on information generated internally, with little regard for external sources. However, in a small number of companies senior staff have started to take on board information management concepts and to recognize the potential such an approach will have on future business success. The impo

SECTION 1
THE REPORT

Background

This report focuses on the relationship between information and business performance. Previous work by Angela Abell in the UK and Dr. Mariam Ginman in Finland investigated the relationship between the 'information culture' of a company and its business performance. Abell and Ginman are members of the 'Åbo Consortium', a loose affiliation of researchers in the UK and the Nordic countries, which also includes Professor Johan Olaisen of the Norwegian Business School and Professor Tom Wilson of the University of Sheffield. The Consortium has met from time to time to discuss the development of a collaborative approach to business information research and the project reported here was intended to serve as a model for parallel investigations to be carried out in other countries.

The report also builds upon previous work in the business information sector, including a number of studies carried out at the University of Sheffield, particularly the investigation of information needs in business by White and Wilson (1987) which used a case study approach.

Abell has drawn a number of conclusions from her review of the literature on information and business performance (Abell and Winterman, 1992):

- the way information is managed and used is very much a product of the culture and management style of the organization;
- changes in organizational structures and methods of using human resources, together with the virtually universal implementation of information technology, could have a significant effect on the way information is perceived and used by organizations;
- current management thinking puts information and cross-functional access to information at the core of business operations;
- an 'adaptive' corporate culture encourages employees to work at their highest achievement level and is able to absorb change. This kind of culture, which is thought necessary for long-term growth, has characteristics in common with an 'information culture';
- information systems are being implemented to gain competitive

advantage: the management of these systems and their content are seen as crucial to their effectiveness;
- corporate know-how, human resources, and information systems are being identified as 'hidden assets' and are now emerging from hiding.

Abell's pilot study of a number of firms used an interview schedule devised by Mariam Ginman for companies in Finland (demonstrating the feasibility of cross-national collaboration). Abell concluded, from the pilot, that information *as a concept* has become a central issue for most firms, but that the interpretation of the concept varies considerably from person to person. Although internal and external information are not necessarily seen as different, the nature of the former and the means for its management and control are more readily understood. There is an increasing interest in information management, but this is generally thought of in relation only to internal information, and the acquisition and effective management of external information are still given little thought in most places.

Literature review

A brief scan of the literature relating to this topic illustrates the enormous amount of work that has been done in this area in recent years. As a background to the present study, this section looks at a sample of this research.

A large number of studies have concentrated on the impact of information technology on business performance. However, information is increasingly seen as a valuable organizational resource for companies. Cronin and Gudmin (1986) stated:

> There is today a widespread appreciation of the value of information as a social and organizational resource. Society has become increasingly dependent on the effective acquisition and use of information, and the means by which these goals are achieved have become key components of the planning and policy making cycle.

They believe information can fall into three categories:

- information
- information technology
- intellectual technology

Information refers to the intellectual product of human cognitive processing; IT is the technical ability to process and transfer the information product; and intellectual technology refers to 'packaged solutions', for example, indexing methods. They see information as an essentially intangible product and therefore very difficult to measure:

> Information seems to have the features of a hidden property good in that its value or contribution to the research or decision making process may not be fully appreciated until long after the moment of consumption or use.

Technology and business performance

The extent to which investments in information technology systems have been able to provide a company with a sustained advantage has been called into question in recent literature. Loveman (1988) states:

> Despite years of impressive technological improvements and investments there is not yet any evidence that information technology is improving productivity or any other measure of business performance.

Venkataraman (1994) believes that there are a number of questions that IT managers must address:

- Is the logical requirement of aligning business and IT (information technology) and IS (information systems) strategies, so compelling just a few years ago, now obsolete?
- Have IT and IS become a common utility that is best managed for efficiency alone?
- Is the role of IT in our business today fundamentally different from its role in the past decade?
- Does IT still play a role in shaping new business strategies, or does it simply play a supporting role in executing current strategies
- What is the source of IT competence: inside our organization or outside through partnerships and alliances?

How well a firm is able to convert spending on information resources such as investment in information systems may depend upon the type of work it is engaged in. Studies that show return on IT investment (Harris and Katz, 1991) have concentrated on traditional information intensive industries, for example the insurance industry.

Studies that have found the opposite to be true have concentrated on manufacturing or information non-intensive industries (Loveman, 1988; Olson and Weill, 1989). Therefore, it is sensible to assume that information intensive industries are more likely to achieve measurably improved performance from investment in information resources.

Olson and Weill (1989) have found that firms differ in their ability to benefit from investment in information resources. They found four internal factors that may contribute to this:

- top management commitment to IT and information investment;
- the organization's previous experience with IT and information systems;
- the organization's previous satisfaction with IT and information systems;
- the extent of political turbulence within the organization.

Within industries other, structural, factors must also be considered when examining why some firms are more effective than others in developing and using information systems effectively. These external factors include:

- the state of the market;
- the financial standing of the firm prior to the introduction of information systems;
- the size of the firm, and its subsequent ability to benefit from economies of scale;
- the nature of the industry, i.e. traditional information intensive industries (banking, insurance, etc.) versus traditional information non-intensive manufacturing industries.

One additional factor that has emerged from this investigation is the nature of the company's growth. In other words, problems can arise when a company has grown through acquisition of an existing company, rather than through organic growth. This has led in a number of cases to the acquisition of information systems that are incompatible with the company's existing information infrastructure.

Banker *et al* (1993) describe four additional internal factors that are considered in the report:

- IT strategy and the company's IT planning process;
- the organization of IT decision making, including policies concerning outsourcing, etc.;
- IT project selection and the processes by which it is done;
- IT project management.

Adler (1989) points to four processes that conceptualize information resource management:

- formulating an information strategy;

- structuring for executing the information strategy;
- pursuing the right IT applications;
- managing IT projects effectively.

Adler defines an IT strategy as 'a pattern of decisions that sets the (IT) goals and the business goals of the organization'. This does not assume that the IT strategy is either written down or widely shared. Some observers have noted that the absence of an explicit or widely shared, written IT strategy is more common than its presence (Beer *et al*, 1990).

If a firm has no explicit strategy it will exhibit a pattern of decisions that reflects its implicit expectations or goals for IT.

> While implicit expectation can affect the firm's IT conversion effectiveness, explicit strategies are more likely to be carried out effectively. (Beer *et al*, 1990)

A key issue in IT and information resource planning is the relationship between a firm's business strategy and its IT and information strategy. Markus and Bjorn-Anderson (1986) have emphasized the importance of this:

> We would further expect IT conversion effectiveness to be higher in firms that have addressed their IT strategy setting process, not only to the applications portfolio, but also to other policy areas related to the execution of IT strategy.

Silk (1988) writes:

> Senior managers are realizing that they need to be more closely involved (in the IT planning process), because IT can now contribute to business strategy.

Silk goes on to say that there are three areas for management education that need to be addressed before they can go on to make important decisions about investment in IT and information systems:

- knowledge of the potential and the limitations of IT;
- knowledge of the information systems now available, and of the legal framework within which they operate;
- skills to assess the information needs of an organization, formulate an information strategy, and deal with specialists implementing new information systems.

He points to three types of player involved in information management issues:

- top manager
- IT professional
- the user

Each player is important and will represent a different level of IT knowledge and education. Silk argues that organizations need to recognize these differences and concentrate resources to educate staff so they are able to make decisions about information resources provision and investments in IT and information systems.

He concludes by saying that information is a strategic issue for management. He found that in practice managers have some difficulty in considering information as a resource alongside other more tangible and measurable resources.

King (1994) points to one of the most important factors of IT strategy planning; that is, the structure of IT services within a firm. Essentially, a firm can take one of two approaches to the structure of its IT provision: the centralized approach, or the decentralized approach. Loveman (1988) believes that too much decentralization can negate benefits from IT investment as it can lead to uncoordinated IT spending. He concludes that all firms can benefit from some form of centralization of information resources.

However, too much centralization can also have negative effects. Markus and Bjorn-Anderson (1986) argue that:

> High centralization allows IT professionals to exert excessive influence over technology acquisition decisions.

Furthermore, they argue that high centralization has historically resulted in restrictions on line managers' authority to engage the services of external IT vendors. The decision to provide centralized or decentralized information resources also raises the issue over in-house development of IT solutions or whether to outsource this function. The introduction of CASE tools have made the in-house option more attractive to IT managers in recent years. But some observers argue that there can be substantial benefits to outsourcing the IT function. DiNardo and Williams (1981) have looked at the banking industry and have concluded that outsourcing can reduce the burden of applications development and the risk of obsolescence.

However, May (1979) argued that in-house processing increases a bank's control over timing and costs to make computing more responsive, to enable customized applications, and to reduce costs per transaction. It is therefore possible to conclude that it is difficult to identify the right level of centralization and the right level of outsourcing to benefit best from investment in IT resources. The companies investigated in the present study have employed various combinations of the solutions described above with differing levels of success.

Porter (1985) points to a lack of willingness in companies to invest in those assets and capabilities that are most required for competitiveness. He writes:

> What is at issue is a much broader problem, involving the entire system of allocating investment capital within and across companies.

Porter argues that firms waste resources on investments with limited financial or social rewards, while they should be investing in employee training and skills development, information systems, organizational development, and closer supplier relationships. He recognizes that these 'softer' investments are important to competition but are also more difficult to measure and evaluate.

Researchers have employed various methods of measuring the rate of return on investments in 'soft' or intangible resources such as information. Cronin and Gudmin (1986) believe the problems of placing a 'value' on information make assessing its contribution to performance very complex. They define productivity as follows:

> At its most basic level, productivity can be described as that state of affairs which exists when the benefits gained from the organization's valuable output of products and services exceed the costs associated with the inputs required to bring about this state of affairs.

Cronin and Gudmin have inferred from their research that despite heavy investment in information systems in recent years productivity in the information sector has not increased proportionately. There are various ways of measuring productivity. Flowerdew and Whitehead (1974) have adopted a cost-benefit approach: they analyze the worth of a policy or project by comparing all its costs with all its benefits. Blair (1986) believes productivity gains can be measured by comparing labour time for ongoing office processes with the same processes after automation.

Segars and Grover (1994) have developed a method of analyzing the industry level impact of IT by using strategic group analysis. They write:

> Lower costs, flexibility and enhanced capabilities afforded by today's information technology (IT) has caused it to evolve from a reactive organizational handyman to a proactive corporate resource capable of distinguishing a firm within its industry.

Information ethos

Other investigations have concentrated on how a company's attitude towards information provision can affect its performance. Mariam Ginman's investigation, *Information Culture and Business Performance* (1988), forms the basis of the present study. Ginman investigated three main aspects of companies' information culture in a business environment:

- The Chief Executive Officer's (CEO) approach to information;
- Company characteristics;
- Personal characteristics of the CEO

She described two development phases that companies go through: chronological development and the company life cycle. The individual phases of chronological development are further defined as:

- initial phase,
- functional phase,
- decentralized phase,
- official supervision phase,
- information phase.

The company life cycle is defined by five phases:

- birth phase,
- growth phase,
- maturity phase,
- revival phase,
- decline phase.

Ginman concluded that a highly developed information culture correlates positively with successful business performance and is closely connected with activities, attitudes, and business cultures initiating successful results. Furthermore she concluded that:

- The supply of information to companies must be designed to comply with their prevailing culture and requirements
- All the different factors must be kept flexible; if a company can move from one phase to another during its life cycle it is in a position to achieve success with a minimum of conflict
- Intellectual resource transformations must be incorporated in strategic planning on an equal footing with the planning of material resources

Abell and Winterman (1992) reviewed the literature relating to corporate information culture. They concluded that:

- Corporate culture has two levels: shared values and group behaviour norms. These influence each other and affect how easy it is to implement change.
- Corporate culture can have a significant impact on a firm's long term performance. Firms which have an appropriate culture outperform those that don't. Also, a performance degrading culture tends to inhibit a firm from changing.

The case study approach has been employed in a number of studies. In 1982 Koenig surveyed four highly productive US pharmaceutical companies and four less productive ones. Koenig found the most successful companies shared five characteristics in their approach to information use:

- greater openness to information;
- less openness when protecting proprietary information;
- greater development of information systems;
- greater end user use of information including browsing and serendipity;
- greater technical and subject sophistication of the information service staff.

A number of studies carried out at Sheffield University have also used the case study approach in investigating the information needs of businesses (White and Wilson, 1987; Roberts and Clarke, 1988). Wilson concluded that:

- It is evident that business people can readily understand the concept of information types and their relevance to the business
- Business people recognize the idea of the strategic significance of information
- External as well as internal information can be seen as significant
- Local or national circumstances may dictate (a) how information types are categorized, and (b) the perceived importance of the different types.

Wilson (1987) found a fuzziness in information needs of business people. He concluded that the information needs of business are of two kinds:

- information needed by individuals to pursue their roles within an organization,
- information needed by the organization, regardless of who is engaged on the organization's behalf.

Abell and Winterman (1992) stated that the terms 'information', 'information culture', 'corporate culture', 'information systems', 'information technology', 'human resources', 'management' and 'organization' are highly interwoven and enmeshed.

The intangible nature of information as a resource makes placing a value on it and then assessing its contribution to performance very complex. Kettinger *et al* (1994) have observed three factors that may affect a firm's ability to achieve sustainable benefit from investment in information resources:

- environmental factors
- foundation factors
- action strategies

Environmental factors that may affect sustainability include unique industry characteristics, changes in regulatory framework, and political changes. Foundation factors include the size of the company and its ability to benefit from economies of scale, and the geographic scope of

the company. The location of a company may result in strategic decisions, for example whether the product and sales facilities are located at
the customer site or at some other advantageous location. The company's
learning curve affects its ability to both acquire and maintain knowledge.
Another important factor is the company's information resources. 'The
richness and content of the firm's knowledge base have been viewed as
a contributor to competitive advantage' (King, 1994). A rich knowledge
base may translate into the development of sophisticated analytical tools
to enhance the service and development of strategic systems.

A body of work emerged in the 1980s which seemed to suggest that
information technology (IT) could provide a company with a distinct
competitive advantage over its rivals (see Porter and Millar, 1985;
Parsons, 1983; McFarlan, 1984).

Organizational structure/culture

The way organizations are structured can affect the success of information systems. Herzog (1994) defines organizational culture as follows:

> Organizational culture encompasses all the corporate
> value systems, policies, authority and decision infrastruc-
> tures and 'historic traditions' that affect how the members
> of the organizations behave.

The development of information systems and the widespread introduction of new technology changes the way organizations are structured.
In order to implement these changes successfully, the organization must
be capable of changing the way it functions.

Successful organizations tend to be those which are successful at
managing these changes. Kotter (1982) has found that organizations
which fail to implement change successfully do so because they commit
some basic errors. Kotter identified eight errors:

- not establishing a great enough sense of urgency;
- not creating a powerful enough guiding coalition;
- lacking a vision;
- undercommunicating the vision by a factor of ten;
- not systematically planning for and creating short-term wins;
- not removing obstacles to the new vision;
- declaring victory too soon;
- not anchoring changes in the corporation's culture.

Successful companies require strong leadership, and a CEO with a clear vision and enthusiasm for change.

Measuring the impact of IT and IS developments

Segars and Grover (1994) believe that the impact of information systems introduced by one company can cross firm boundaries and affect the very nature of the firm's industry structure. Bakos (1991) noted that:

> Literature in the area abounds with a number of frameworks for identifying and categorizing opportunities. There has been a notable absence, however, of testable models based on relevant theory. As this area of research matures, there is an increasing need to move beyond frameworks and toward exploratory models of the underlying phenomena.

Segars and Grover believe their methodology goes some way towards redressing the balance by focusing on the industry level impact of technology, as opposed to the in-firm impact that has formed the basis of case study projects in the past. They believe there are six specific issues that need to be addressed by managers in organizations that wish to develop effective information systems:

- How can managers assess the sustainability of applications designed for competitive advantage? How long before a response? Which competitors can respond? How effective will this response be?
- When is adoption of IT a competitive necessity?
- What enables a particular company to succeed with IT based strategy whilst others in the sector fail?
- What factors facilitate the use of IT for competitive advantage?
- What are the competitive risks of developing strategic information systems?
- When can an IT based strategy confer competitive advantage?

There are a number of other models that measure the business success of companies. These include the European and UK Total Quality of Management Award models, the *Most Admired Company* Studies and the British Quality of Management Award.

The European and UK Total Quality of Management Award models were developed by over 400 managers in Europe. The models measure factors that fall into two broad categories: enabler factors and results factors. Enabler factors include: leadership, policy strategy, process management, resource management, and people management. Results factors include: people satisfaction, customer satisfaction, impact on society, and business results.

The *Most Admired Company* Studies (Saunders *et al*, 1992) have measured the following factors: quality of management, financial soundness, quality of products and services, the ability to attract, develop and retain top talent, value as a long term investment, capacity to innovate, quality of marketing, community and environmental responsibility, and the use of corporate assets.

The British Quality of Management Award focuses on the following factors: strategic thinking, leadership, investment plans, management skills, research and development, innovation, culture, responsive information, dynamism, technology, team, people, brand, and market research.

It is interesting to note that only one model mentions the importance of using information provision as a measure of a company's success.

The research presented here is meant to serve as an introduction to a varied subject that has attracted the attention of a wide variety of researchers in recent years. It is the aim of the present project to go some way towards addressing some of the topics raised in this review of literature.

Methodology

The project

The aim of this project was to explore the relationship between the business performance of companies and various 'information-related' variables, according to a theoretical model.

As a result of a number of discussions within the Åbo Consortium, a model of the relationship between company performance and other factors was evolved for the research proposal and is shown in Figure 1.

Figure 1

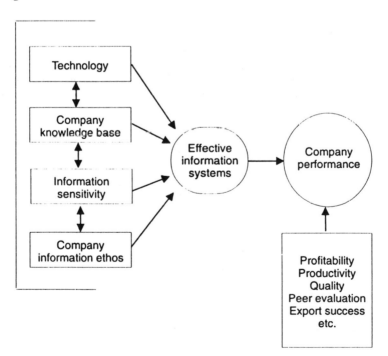

In the diagram, 'information sensitivity' and 'company information ethos' are related to Abell and Ginman's 'information culture' (Abell and Winterman, 1992; Ginman, 1988). Information sensitivity is defined by the extent to which organizational members are able to discriminate between different kinds of information, their view of the relationship between internal and external information resources, and the sophistication of their understanding of the concept of information management. Corporate information ethos is assessed by the extent to which information systems and services are seen as central to business performance, systems for the acquisition of external information are in place, and the value of information is perceived and promulgated throughout the firm.

Particular attention was paid in the study to:

- the ways in which information technology is used to deliver information services, covering both internal and external information and data;
- what constitutes the knowledge base;
- how far the knowledge base is at risk through dependency on individuals rather than systems;
- how sensitive key company staff are to the value of information as a contributor to performance;
- how far the company can be described as having an information ethos, through which the value of information is conveyed to all workers.

Information on these variables was linked to assessment of how effective information systems were perceived by organizational members to be in delivering quality information.

The overall methodology employed was that of the case study. As the study focuses specifically on how 'high performing' companies use information systems it was felt that the case study approach would provide a firm-level perspective on the issues many companies face in designing effective information systems.

The case studies are based on qualitative data collected through a series of interviews with key staff members in the selected organizations. These were followed by a self-completed questionnaire (see Appendix 2), distributed to a more representative selection of staff to see how the views of key staff were reflected in the organization as a whole.

Selection of participants

The selection criteria sought to identify British companies that can be described as 'high performing', using a combination of financial and non-financial measures. Figure 1 sets out the factors which contribute to business performance and which were used as the selection criteria:

- Profitability
- Productivity
- Quality
- Peer evaluation
- Export success

The companies had to fulfil a number of the following conditions to meet these criteria:

- have industry quartiles in the median or upper classifications;
- appear in the *Times 500* list of profitable companies;
- appear in the *Euro 500* list of companies, as published in *Management Today*;
- appear in the *Britain's Most Admired Company* study (Saunders *et al,* 1992).

During the selection process effort was made to include companies from sectors that have been affected by the recent recession, such as the manufacturing and building industries. Effort was also made to select several companies from the newly privatized utilities (e.g. water and electricity) and from sectors that had been affected by government legislation, such as the recently deregulated television and financial sectors. Additional financial measures used include turnover, profitability, and market share.

Following the selection procedure twenty-five companies from a range of industrial sectors were contacted to be included in this study. The sectors covered are: manufacturing, media, leisure, retail, financial, water and electricity. Following the contact procedure, twelve companies agreed to take part in the project, distributed as shown in Table 1.

Table 1: Description of case companies

Company	Description
Company A	Water Provider
Company B	Building Society
Company C	Television Company
Company D	Dairy and Food Producer/Wholesaler
Company E	High Street Bank
Company F	Glass Manufacturer
Company G	Fashion Retailer
Company H	Life Insurance Company
Company I	Computer Hardware/Software Company
Company J	Leisure/ Brewing Company
Company K	Auto-repair Company
Company L	Cosmetic Manufacturer/Retailer

Company ranking by primary UK SIC code and sales

Using Dialog's File 562, British Financial Data Sheets, the companies were ranked by their individual primary SIC codes and sorted by sales. Table 2 shows the relevant position of each company in terms of sales within their individual market sectors.

Of the twelve companies, seven are in the top ten when ranked by primary SIC and sales. This measurement does not apply to three companies (company B, company E, and company H). Of the remaining two companies, one is ranked 21st, the other 11th. In other words, most of the twelve companies are in a similar position in their own market in terms of performance measured by sales. Company K is ranked 21st partly because a number of its subsidiary companies based overseas have been adversely affected by the world recession. Thus, the majority of the companies can be described as 'high performing' in terms of total sales.

Another way of looking at the companies is to split them along information intensive and information non-intensive lines. This is useful because previous studies have discovered that a firm's ability to benefit from information and information systems is in part due to the nature of the business it is engaged in. For example, studies of information

Table 2: *Sales positions of the case companies*

Company	Position
Company A	1st
Company B	N/A
Company C	4th
Company D	2nd
Company E	N/A
Company F	1st
Company G	3rd
Company H	N/A
Company I	11th
Company J	6th
Company K	21st
Company L	5th

intensive industries, such as banking or insurance (Bender, 1986), have shown a high return on IT investment. Studies of information non-intensive industries, such as heavy manufacturing (Loveman, 1988; Olson and Weill, 1989), have found little or no benefit from IT investment. Table 3 shows how the twelve companies can be split along these lines.

Table 3: *Information intensity of case companies*

Information intensive		Information non-intensive	
Company B	Building Society	Company A	Water Provider
Company C	Television Company	Company D	Dairy Food Producer/ Wholesaler
Company E	High street Bank	Company F	Glass Manufacturer
Company G	Fashion Retailer	Company I	Computer Hardware/ Software Company
Company H	Life Insurance Company	Company J	Leisure/Brewing Company
Company L	Cosmetic Manufacturer/ Retailer	Company K	Auto-repair Company

A number of companies described as information non-intensive are increasingly moving towards becoming information intensive. This change is occurring as companies are placing more emphasis on collecting information about their customers. These companies are also more likely to benefit from the introduction of inter-organizational information systems; for example, by linking their company with its main suppliers using Electronic Data Interchange (EDI) systems, and by linking sales outlets with company headquarters using Electronic Point of Sales (EPOS) systems.

The contact procedure

After some discussion a contact letter was drafted and sent to twenty-five companies. The letters were addressed to the Heads of Public Relations Departments, or people holding a similar position. The initial response yielded three positive replies, six negative replies, and one company that was considering the request. The negative replies came from some of the country's largest companies. The common reason for not taking part was the number of similar requests received by the companies and the difficulty in identifying the appropriate people who would be best placed to respond to the investigation.

A reminder letter was sent to those companies that had failed to respond to the original approach. The reminder letter yielded five positive responses, and four negative responses. Following the two letters, six companies had failed to respond in any way, and one company was still considering its response.

The researcher contacted the seven companies by telephone, speaking in the first instance to the original recipient of the contact letters. Three of these companies claimed never to have received either of the original contact letters; one stated that it was company policy not to participate in external research projects. The remainder had passed the letters on to the Information Systems or Information Technology departments of the company. The researcher then attempted to contact the people to whom the letters had been passed.

In total, the initial contact procedure had produced eight positive responses. The project team felt this was too small a sample, so a third letter was drafted to be sent to the Chief Executive Officer of those companies that had either rejected the initial contacts, or who had failed to reply. This procedure was repeated a number of times until a satisfactory response was achieved.

The contact procedure outlined above produced twelve positive responses. The original proposal called for a sample group of between twelve and twenty companies.

Problems

Making contact with selected companies and securing their cooperation proved to be a very time consuming process. Some of the problems encountered by the researcher are described in this section.

The company addresses and telephone numbers were obtained from Dun and Bradstreet's *Company Information Directory*. The researcher telephoned the switchboard of each company and obtained the name of the Head of the Public Relations Department, or the equivalent. It was more difficult actually to speak to the recipients of the contact letters. Phone calls were usually answered by the secretary who would take a message, but would rarely put the researcher through to the contact. When the researcher managed to speak with the recipients of the letters they were, in general, quite helpful. Many had passed the letters on to other departments within the organization.

The timing of the contact phase presented some problems. A number of company contacts were on holiday during this time. As a result, the contact phase took more time than the project team had anticipated. Another problem was obtaining the cooperation of more than one representative in the organization. In only two instances did more than one representative agree to be interviewed. Linked to this was the difficulty in obtaining an adequate return of the questionnaires distributed in the organizations; this will be discussed in a later section.

Adding to the problems described above is the difficulty in conducting research which requires a degree of cooperation from industry in a difficult economic climate. One negative reply from a large media corporation illustrates this:

> ... we get a large number of such requests and are simply unable to do justice to them as well as do the jobs we are paid to do.

Linked to this is the importance of pointing out to the organizations the benefits to them of participating in the research. One negative reply from a large retail chain-store stated:

> ...[we have] taken the view that we will only respond to

> those [projects] which are likely to result in real benefits
> to the company.

One further problem was that the original contact letters were immediately passed to the Information Services or Information Systems Department of the organization. While it was useful to discuss the topics with information specialists, it would have been better to get a range of opinions from across the business functions, from the actual users of the information systems. The researcher had no real idea of the structure of the organizations contacted, and therefore had to rely on the initial recipient of the contact letter to forward it to appropriate departments. However, as the letter stated that the area of research was information and information systems, the original recipient naturally forwarded the letter to the departments responsible for this.

The researcher attempted to contact representatives from other business functions in the organizations that had agreed to participate. This proved to be unsuccessful; in general, the person who agreed to take part in the survey felt other members of staff would be unwilling to devote any time to the project.

However, having stated these problems, the majority of organizations that agreed to take part in the project did so willingly. This may be because some organizations have already started thinking about the information management topics that are examined in the project, and feel the conclusions will be of use to the organization.

Questionnaire distribution

In addition to the interview conducted with one or more representatives from the selected companies a self-completed questionnaire was prepared (see Appendix 2). The questionnaire followed closely the topics in the interview schedule. The interviews were conducted with senior staff, and the questionnaire was to be circulated among other staff members to gain a more qualitative perception of the extent to which the views of senior staff were represented in the organization at large.

The researcher distributed the questionnaires through the interviewee(s). In all, ten copies of the questionnaire were distributed within each of the participating organizations. The questionnaires were supplied with stamped return envelopes and the interviewees were instructed to pass them to staff who would be likely to complete and return them.

The rate of return varied widely depending on the organization concerned. Reminder letters were sent to the companies. This increased the return rate, but the resulting sample of 35 per cent was rather disappointing, although not unusual in organizational research.

A telephone interview schedule was constructed based on the original interview schedule. The researcher then contacted information professionals within the selected companies and telephone interviews were conducted with information staff in six of the companies.

Results

The interviews and the subsequent analysis of the questionnaire returns produced a great deal of qualitative data. In order to analyze this data it is useful to refer back to the Åbo Consortium performance model (see Figure 1 on p.17). The data collected were analyzed within the framework of this model. This analysis concentrated on the variables which lead into effective information systems, namely:

- technology
- company knowledge base
- information sensitivity
- company information ethos
- organization structure/culture

An attempt was then made to determine to what extent the organizations surveyed had developed effective information systems.

Technology

All companies had invested heavily in information technology as a delivery mechanism for information provision. However, the companies approached information technology provision in different ways. Figure 2 shows how useful the companies have found certain new technologies to be in delivering information effectively.

It is clear that the majority of companies use electronic mail (e-mail) to communicate information. One interviewee stated that e-mail is now the common means of information transfer within the company. Other developments such as inter-organizational EDI systems have been useful to some of the manufacturing companies, but are not used in the majority of companies surveyed.

Expert systems are effective where they are used. Most companies are wary of applying emerging technologies to their business. They prefer to wait for the technologies to be proven useful by their competitors before making the investment. This attitude is illustrated by a comment from a manager in company D, who said:

Figure 2: *How effective are the following in providing information solutions?*

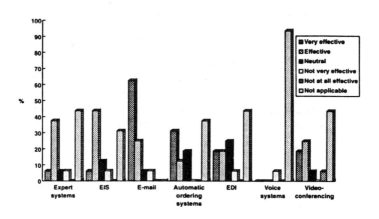

Let someone else prove the technology, prove its worth and prove the benefits it can have to the business.

When asked about expert systems Company B explained why these were not being used:

.... it's not failings in the technology, it's somewhere between cultural failings within our own staff and within our customers.

IT and business success

A number of the companies attributed their success to their IT investments. A representative from company A stated :

It's a major competitive advantage for us in the way that we've implemented and managed our use of information technology.

Company E has invested heavily in IT; several representatives explained why:

> Banking is totally an IT driven industry and it's key, absolutely key, to the way it works..

Another manager from Company E elaborated on this statement:

> ... the key to keeping alive is product innovation, speed of change, satisfying customers; and all that comes back to IT at the end of the day. Giving you summaries of information on your customers, what their habits are, if your products are right, all these sorts of things...

A third manager explained:

> Banking, many people say, is just about processing information, and if we are not the most effective processors of financial information we will find ourselves shut out of the market place by people who *can* effectively process information.

The success of IT in providing information systems has also been linked to the degree of top management commitment to IT and to managers' ability to implement change successfully. A representative from Company A illustrated this point. He stated:

> ...in information technology we've also done an incredible amount. I think from the CEO down we've created an environment, a culture, in which you can implement and use IT in a very effective way.

Company B feels its information technology is beneficial to the success of the company because it is closely aligned to the needs of the business functions. This has been achieved by actively involving these functions in the planning and design process. The director of business information systems explained:

> We've demystified the systems development process to the point where those who really understand the information needs at the sharp end of the application have the biggest say in what the application does.

This approach to information systems development was mirrored in the other companies surveyed. For example, Company H stated:

> The important factor [in information systems develop-
> ment] is that the project sponsor owns the benefits and is
> responsible for delivering the benefits.

This is also illustrated in Figure 3.

*Figure 3: How effectively are your information systems designed to
achieve your key business objectives?*

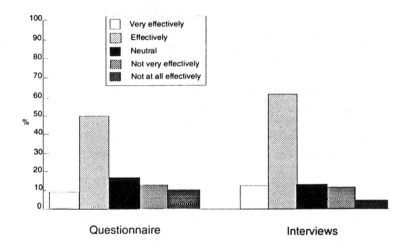

As we can see, the majority of the companies surveyed believe their
information systems are designed to achieve business objectives and that
they do this effectively.

A number of the companies felt their existing IT and information
systems were a barrier to success. A significant proportion of those
surveyed had grown through acquiring existing businesses, rather than
through purely organic growth. In this way they had acquired a number
of legacy systems that are now outdated and expensive to operate.
Company H stated that:

A key element of the existing information systems strategy is to reduce the number of legacy systems which we operate.

A representative from Company B explained why he felt their current information systems were a barrier to success:

.... our current information systems solutions provide us with a significant disadvantage in relation to our key competitors. That is all to do with their cost-effectiveness; most of our mainstream products and services are approaching commodity status. A mortgage is a mortgage is a mortgage. As such, what we need (and this is our corporate strategy) is to achieve low cost production, as the saying will go. We need to be able to sell and service a mortgage account for as little cost as possible. Then we can either price our product, i.e. the interest rate we have to charge can be better than some of our competitors with higher expenses, or we can charge the same and make more profit. Either way we should drive our cost base down. As a legacy of some of our current systems, they are less cost-effective solutions than they ought to be.

Evaluation of IT and IS

One problem that was almost universally acknowledged was the general lack of evaluation procedures once an information system was in place. A number of the companies explained that no formal evaluation procedure existed because if a particular system failed to produce the perceived benefits then it was immediately apparent. For example a senior manager in Company G stated:

If they don't bloody work someone gets kicked in the teeth.

However, the majority of companies surveyed did feel they needed a formal evaluation process. Lack of finances and lack of time were the common reasons for their failure to evaluate the success of information systems in the past.

IT and company libraries

In the companies where library staff were surveyed it was apparent that they were slow to embrace new technology. While the majority did have computer-based catalogues, many of these were on stand-alone machines. Therefore, access was available only in the library itself. Company F did not have its catalogue available electronically. The librarian explained:

> The library isn't catalogued on computer yet; again that's something we want to do when we get the money and the people to do it.

The library in Company B supplies a feed into the executive information system, as does Company A. A number of the company librarians interviewed did play a small part in information systems provision. The only occasions library staff did become involved in this area was in the purchasing or design of information systems for the library function itself.

A number of the companies with libraries had CD-ROM readers and subscribed to a small number of CD-ROM titles. Company C has no CD-ROM facilities, although the librarian felt this would be useful. Company F has CD-ROM facilities but made little use of CD-ROMs. All companies made use of online sources of information, with *FT Profile* being the most popular. Other online services include *Dialog*, *Datastar* and *Reuters*. Of all the companies surveyed Company A has embraced IT most effectively. A senior manager commented:

> I think the important thing about the library itself is the way it's used. Again, five years ago the library mainly dealt with giving people pieces of paper. Nowadays a lot of their work is done by doing electronic data searches in external libraries, electronic libraries.

Company knowledge base

An attempt was made to identify what constitutes the knowledge base of the companies surveyed. The extent to which this knowledge base is at risk through dependency on individuals rather than on systems was also assessed.

A number of companies had developed information systems to store and access their knowledge base. Company I had started a pilot programme which involved extracting information from a number of different systems and putting them into a standard hypertext format using hypertext mark-up language (HTML). This system, known as 'Repository', used the hypertext browser MOSAIC to view the interlinked documents. Although it was still in the initial phase of testing, senior staff thought it was very effective.

Other companies had executive information systems (EIS) or management information systems to enable senior staff to access the company knowledge base. A small number of the companies surveyed identified problems with these systems. A representative from Company E said that all too often EIS suffered from what he called 'the comic book effect'. In other words, he felt that so much emphasis was placed on the graphical representation of data that the value of the data was lost.

Other criticisms of EIS were that the original source of the data may not be immediately apparent. In this way the lines between information generated internally and external information were often blurred.

Information resources

Another important component of the knowledge base was identified as the company library or information centre. A small number of representatives from these facilities agreed to take part in this project. In total, five library or information professionals were surveyed, from Companies A, B, C, E, and F. Of the remaining seven, three had libraries but the library personnel declined to be interviewed, and four had no library or central information facilities.

As we have seen from the previous section, the libraries were in general rather slow to take up new technology. This was not always due to the reluctance of library personnel. Rather, the main reason was lack of finance and lack of trained personnel. Exceptions to this were Company A and Company B. A senior member of the library staff in Company B described his role as follows:

> I see my role as an information provider not only [through] the library ... but also in terms of wider distribution of management information which I'm personally responsible for. We actually have electronic means of distribution for our management information reports.

The library in Company B provides information to the company EIS and the head of the library acted as project manager for the implementation and design of the library's information systems.

In general the libraries had all seen their budgets cut in recent years. This has caused them to reduce their levels of service and has made them reluctant to promote their activities within the company. This can be illustrated by the following quotes from Company A and Company B:

> Basically we've found that the library hasn't been that well supported in the past in terms of budgets, manning and so on... We haven't necessarily gone out very strongly and advertised our presence.

and:

> We don't often make a public display of saying we do this or we do that. The people who need the information generally know it's ours.

The library in Company F has also suffered cuts in recent years. The chief librarian explained why:

> I think we've just about reached that point, much more cutting back and it just won't be worth carrying on. The recent recession has been hard to us and, being a service department, we usually cop it first.

It seems as though the company libraries are suffering because they are viewed as service departments, sitting on the edge of the organization. All the library staff surveyed recognized the value to the company of the information they provide; and all the staff felt they could do a lot more. The head of the library in Company A said:

> ...we've got documented examples of where raw data that we've provided has been used in presentations and has saved the company a considerable amount of money.

The libraries generally offered a similar range of services to a similar user base. The majority of the work of all libraries surveyed involved maintaining journal collections and internal company reports. The main users of the libraries came from the marketing, planning and sales functions with other users from the directorate or corporate management functions.

Companies A, B, E, and F also circulate some information in the form of current awareness bulletins or current awareness briefings which are included in company magazines. Company F used to provide a selective dissemination of information (SDI) service which was very popular, but this was discontinued due to a lack of staff.

Knowledge base and individuals

The majority of companies surveyed felt that the firm's knowledge base resided in the accumulated knowledge and expertise of their staff. Representatives from companies A, B, G, E and L noted the danger of allowing information pockets to build up and of staff who see themselves as 'information gurus'. A senior manager from Company E described this danger:

> They use this as a means of power within an organization, being the source of all knowledge on a particular thing.

A representative from Company L commented:

> What you inevitably have is little information pockets developing. I don't know of any company who would ever not raise that particular issue.

This attitude was also found in Company B; one manager commented:

> There are some who still work to the philosophy that knowledge is power. You will come across that in other companies. It's an outmoded attitude, and every now and then you still find it...

This highlights some of the dangers of having a company knowledge base that relies too heavily on individuals rather than on systems.

A related problem was highlighted by Company C, which has reduced its labour force in recent years, causing the firm's knowledge base to diminish as expert staff leave. A representative from the company explained why it was difficult to systematize knowledge:

> In the current climate any attempt to extract information from people will be a struggle. People would see it as another means of reducing the number of staff.

Another, almost universal, problem was that of locating which department or which individual had the information staff required. Senior staff used their experience of the organization to identify information pockets, but staff who were relatively new to the organization had found this difficult and time consuming. A representative from Company J said:

> ... they don't tell you who has the information and you can spend a fair bit of time going from pillar to post searching for it ...

Company L felt that its knowledge base would inevitably depend on individuals rather than on systems. A senior manager explained why:

> Knowledge transfer depends on individuals ... we are a relatively young company.. young companies by definition tend to be structured around people rather than functions.

Company G also believed that to have the knowledge base dependent on individuals was a good thing for them at this stage in the company's life. Company G is also relatively young; operating in the fashion industry, it feels its success is due to the creativity of its designers and the business knowledge of its managers and sales force.

Company I highlighted another problem they associated with having a knowledge base too dependent on individuals. One of their main business areas is computer consultancy. This means that experienced staff are required to spend long periods of time working outside the company's main office sites and, consequently, the company's knowledge base is spread over a large geographic area. Therefore, the firm is concentrating on ways to improve communications, rather than systematizing the knowledge itself. A manager described some of the ways the new communications system benefited the company:

> Every single building in [Company I], even the one in Manchester, is on the same telephone exchange. That means we can talk to each other at zero cost (there are some fixed costs for the line), all the time without any hassle. Our data network means we can exchange files with each other, send mail messages, whatever it is you want to do, several times a day, instead of a paper mail cycle of two to three days.

Knowledge base and IS

Company A is undertaking a major project designed to systematize its knowledge base in order to overcome some of the problems which have affected it in the past. A company manager explained one of the aims of this project:

> Where I think the major systematic difference is in terms of expert knowledge ... we are now starting more and more to systematize this knowledge.

The project itself is designed to create rule sets that can be integrated together with other information into systems. The project is managed by the Business Information Systems Department and is part of an overall strategy designed to reorganize the company. The project team described the process as follows:

> We go into different functions within the company and ask a number of questions. Whereas in the past we might ask 'What do you do?', our modelling people and the people who are now more business oriented are asking 'Why do you do that?'. And the difference is important, because we're after the rule sets that people use... Actually starting to try and understand why things work, and build it into the model that we're starting to define now, is an enormous breakthrough in terms of getting the information together.

Two of the companies surveyed have attempted similar projects. Company B and Company E have experimented with expert systems and knowledge based systems to perform routine tasks, such as credit checking customers. These experiments have been successful, but the systems themselves have not been implemented, due to pressure from within the companies and from their customers who preferred the tasks to be completed manually. The companies were also wary of industry regulators who may prevent the introduction of such systems.

The remaining companies surveyed acknowledge the problems associated with a knowledge base which relies on individuals rather than on systems. However, there appears to be no immediate plans to change the situation.

Information sensitivity

In order to assess the information sensitivity of key staff a number of questions were asked. Before describing the results of these questions, it is important to define what we mean by the term 'information sensitivity'.

Information sensitivity is defined by the extent to which senior staff are able to discriminate between internal and external information, and their view of the relationship between internal and external information resources. Linked to this is the sophistication of their understanding of the concept of information management.

Information management

Company A demonstrated a desire to introduce information management concepts to the organization. They admitted they had some problems understanding information management concepts, as one senior manager commented:

> What is the difference between running a data processing department and an information systems department? We did that very successfully. But what is the difference between running an information systems department and an information management function? That is a bigger jump.

One of the problems facing company A is that it is using the same staff who ran the data processing department to organize the information management function. They admitted that some of the staff found it difficult to come to terms with information management concepts.

Monitoring systems

All the companies surveyed had mechanisms in place to monitor various aspects of their own performance, the performance of their main competitors and changes in the market in general. Figure 4 illustrates how effectively the companies surveyed felt this was done.

Figure 4 clearly illustrates the emphasis all companies put on collecting internal information and on monitoring information about the performance of their own company. To some extent it might be expected that 'high performing' companies do not feel it important to devote a

Figure 4: How effectively do your information systems enable you to monitor the following?

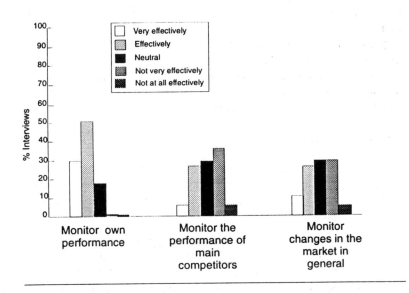

great deal of time and resources to monitoring their competitors. A number of the companies surveyed did not feel they had any direct competitors. For example, Company K stated:

> In some respects we don't need to know exactly what other companies are up to. The company sees itself as the market leader. Therefore, other people follow us, instead of the other way round.

The companies that could identify direct, like-for-like competitors had information systems to monitor their performance. A representative from Company B stated:

> In terms of monitoring the performance of competitors this is a difficult one, because we invest a lot of effort in this. But we are probably far more effective at monitoring the performance of our broad-scale competitors... rather than that of niche players.

Several companies mentioned the perceived threat of new entrants to their market, of niche competitors. Niche competitors are defined as those companies which compete against one or more of the company's products or services. The companies in the financial sector were particularly concerned about niche competitors. A representative from Company E explained:

> ... if you look at the range of products a company like us delivers, there's other people chipping away at it saying, 'we can do this stuff as well'.

Another senior manager in Company E elaborated:

> They're all trying to nip in on the things we're good at, but we've got a big infrastructure behind us in which we've invested heavily, and we've got the branch network ... They are more IT involved and a lot cheaper operation, and they're not going away.

This point was also raised by a manager in Company B, who stated:

> I'm inclined to put 'Not very effectively' [on a response card] for... niche competitors. The point I'm making there, and we do recognize this, is that's a vulnerability, because today they may be a niche competitor, but tomorrow they may be a mainstream competitor... and I think our monitoring systems are not as well geared to spotting the... shooting stars in the industry.

With few exceptions all the companies stated their information systems were either 'effective' or 'very effective' at monitoring their own performance. These systems concentrated on collecting financial information about the companies' operations. A senior manager in Company I stated:

> I do think our financial systems, which are all computerized, do actually help us to monitor our own performance very effectively ... We've put an awful lot of money and time and effort over the 25 years into building our financial reporting systems.

In terms of monitoring changes in the market in general the results were rather mixed. On the whole, the financial companies in the sample believed they monitored this effectively. A representative from Company B said:

> The reason I think we're very effective is not particularly because we're very good at it, but frankly the sources of information that are germane to obtaining that understanding are relatively fulsome and relatively freely available, in that you don't have to spend as much work as you do on gathering competitive information to gather overall market or economic information.

Company L argued that monitoring changes in the market from the point of view of their products is less dependent on monitoring financial indicators. A representative explained:

> I would argue that, whether it's the job of information systems or intelligence systems (I wouldn't argue, I know), the forces, or changes, or consequences that are implicit in the entire demographic change are extremely important, and that is especially true in the US. By that I mean the changing age profile, the ageing of the population. That's not really the job of information systems as such, it's more people being aware, constantly aware of it.

Company L's systems for monitoring its own performance also included aspects other than financial indicators. This company was almost alone in monitoring the impact of its activities on the environment and on the community. The company had brought in an external agency to conduct a social audit on its operations.

Other companies surveyed also monitored non-financial aspects of their operations. Company B and the other financial industry organizations had mechanisms to monitor changes in the regulatory framework which govern their operations. A representative from Company B said:

> Information and intelligence on changes in the regulatory framework... we have to be both very conscious of, and indeed wary of ensuring that we do comply with regulations effectively, and managing to ensure compliance.

These companies also monitored political and other social changes that may impact on their business. Company G monitored changes in demographics and changes in fashions. This information was obtained from a number of sources. In general the marketing departments provided this information to the company.

Internal and external information flow

The majority of the firms surveyed had mechanisms to enable the circulation of internal information and, to some extent, external information, around their company. Although a large proportion of this consists of paper circulation, a number of the companies were moving more and more towards electronic means.

The information circulated tended to be that relating to their own performance and activities. A representative from Company C described a 'scatter-gun' approach, with too much information being circulated to too many people. However, Company C does communicate information electronically in a more orderly fashion. The company has an in-house teletext system which displays information about the company on television screens located in a number of sites. External information circulated within the company is limited to press cuttings which are circulated on a daily basis.

Where information is circulated electronically, the delivery mechanism is mostly by e-mail. Company A circulates information on disc to senior staff. This is called 'Key Facts and Indicators' and contains information collected by the marketing department which scans a variety of sources. Most of the information comes from newspaper and journal clippings about the company's activities.

Company L has its own television company which produces informative films about the company's activities and ethos. These videos are shown to staff in the head office and are circulated to the company's franchised stores around the world. Within its head office the company has a very open approach to information dissemination. One senior director commented:

> We tend to have a policy of very open communication, extremely extensive use of e-mail. We're trying to cut paper out, in fact we're actually in the process of reducing our paper consumption.

The company has a central communications department which is responsible for collecting and disseminating this information. There is also a member of staff, acting as a communicator in each department, who is responsible for ensuring information is disseminated. The company also communicates information verbally, through regular meetings with all staff members.

Company H circulates information at a number of levels. On a formal level individual departments have monthly briefings to ensure that internal information in the business is cascaded down through the various levels of management to every member of staff. The company also uses e-mail to circulate information around the company. One senior manager stated:

> In fact e-mail's used a lot for chucking information around the company, both for business information and social information.

External information is collected by the marketing department which scans trade papers and circulates items relating to the company on a fortnightly basis. Individuals in each department will also scan journals and newspapers and circulate items of interest.

Company G circulates internal information on a regular basis. This consists of paper-based reports containing sales information. External information is circulated informally; individuals take copies of any articles or news items of interest and pass these on to colleagues.

Company K circulates internal information about its own performance on a regular basis. On the whole this is paper-based with financial reports circulated on a daily basis. Managers also receive on-request information, provided in paper form or electronically. Very little external information is circulated within the company. A senior manager could only recall one occasion when he received any external information, this was a report comparing the company's sales against the rest of the industry. The manager found this information useful, but he noted that the exercise was never repeated. Company K has no mechanisms for automatically circulating either internal or external information around the company. Information is available, but it is left to individuals to request information as it is required.

Company D circulates information about its performance on a regular basis. Financial reports containing sales information are circulated on a weekly basis. Information tends to be circulated on paper; e-mail is used on a very limited basis. External information is not circulated.

Company J also circulates information about its performance. A senior manager stated:

> ... we get things circulated every day. Most of it's company

results, results from across the group as a whole, and from individual businesses. Some of this is done via e-mail, but we still get a lot of paper feeds; stuff goes to key individuals within the company.

The same manager commented:

External information is [circulated] purely at the discretion of the individual managers concerned. It's all based on what they consider the people in their department need to know.

Company B has more effective systems for distributing both internal and external information. It uses e-mail to disseminate internal information: general internal information is posted on an electronic bulletin board which can be accessed by all staff members; more specific information aimed at certain catchment groups is e-mailed to these groups using distribution lists. In other words, internal distribution mechanisms are system supported.

External information comes from a variety of sources. Departments within the company subscribe to journals which are circulated on paper. Electronic information sources include CD-ROMs and the use of online information services. Managers also actively seek information on their own initiative through informal 'networking'. One senior manager commented:

... if I go to a one day conference on the effective development of telebanking service ... part of the reason I'm there is to talk to my peers, perhaps in other companies, and I learn a lot about what they are doing.

Some of this 'networking' can be quite formal and organized. For example, a senior manager stated:

... every six months the heads of information services of the top fifteen companies get together for a meeting. Yes, we're all competitors, but we do exchange quite a lot of information with each other about what we're doing and so on... As well as getting involved in organizations like the Building Society Association, the Council of Mortgage Lenders, and so on.

Company I uses IT to some extent in disseminating information around the company. The company uses e-mail to produce internal mailing lists which staff can subscribe to, and to disseminate general company information. The company also has an electronic news interface and internal company discussion groups. The information communicated in this way tends to concentrate on internally generated information, although the company does circulate externally produced scientific and technical reports. One problem with electronic circulation of information is that the company is spread across a huge geographic area. At the present time the company's information network covers the whole of the UK and some parts of the US. The company is currently examining ways to improve this and extend its network to cover all of its operations.

Information ethos

This section examines how far the companies surveyed can be described as having an information ethos, through which the value of information is conveyed to all workers. This is an area highlighted in recent literature as important in assuring business success (Abell and Winterman, 1992; Ginman, 1988).

The companies surveyed varied in the degree to which an information ethos could be identified by staff members. This is illustrated in Figure 5. Interestingly, senior staff found it more difficult to identify an information ethos than did other staff members.

However, senior staff from a number of companies surveyed could either identify an information ethos or culture in their organizations, or were actively working towards developing one. When questioned on this a senior representative from Company L stated:

> I think I've answered that already in terms of the emphasis placed on the very open interchange of information, the communication with everyone from the shop floor level... Members of the executive team .. leave the information in people's hands. There's a very proactive approach which is very much to do with our ethos; there's a very proactive approach to employee communications, an openness on most issues, on all issues.

Company A is in the process of developing an information ethos which will run through its operations. A senior manager at the company described this process:

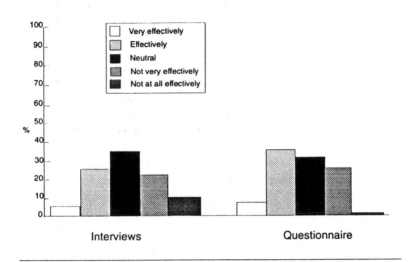

Figure 5: How effectively do you think the company's attitude towards information ensures the value of information is conveyed to all workers?

We're trying to get the message across to everybody. At the moment we're doing a systems strategy in the new business teams and the operational groups we've set up. But we aren't calling it an information systems strategy, we're calling it an information strategy. Because the guys in there said: 'We don't want to know about systems and computers, we want to know about information'. So in almost all the business areas we're starting to focus on, we want to manage information. That means you've got to relate it to your business need, what you want it for; the context I've put it in, and the decisions I make with it. I think that's where we're starting to come at it, much more in terms of how we use information.

Company B is embarked on a similar process. Senior managers recognize the value of information and are attempting to create a facul-tative management style in the company which is conducive to the open communication of information to staff at all levels. A senior manager elaborated on this process:

> We do recognize that information is an asset, and therefore we should maximize the value from that asset, and make it available to all those who can obtain value from it. We are working on the devolution of decision making responsibility. We talk a lot about flattening the organization structure, and we have achieved a certain amount of progress. I think we've got the right attitude, but we're still going through a learning process. I believe the more enlightened managers understand that a facultative management style is the right style for modern business practice; that staff working in the business processes are best placed to make these processes effective, and these are the ones who really need the information.

Senior staff in Company D identified this as one area which could be improved. The director of information systems in Company D stated:

> I think there are certain elements of information like profit performance, that's all the financial indicators, where that culture runs through the business. In relation to other information I don't think we do it very well. I've taken on this role as head of information systems to try and provide a catalyst for doing that, rather than have somebody that's an IT expert running the department. Well I've still got a department to run. I think information and systems are as important as the technology, if not more so. We therefore need to find ways and means of letting people know what's available as well as talking to them about what I think they ought to know. Do you know this, do you not think it's important? As opposed to: I don't know, why should I know?.

A distinction was made between proactive staff who are already aware of the information resources available to them, and other staff who are prepared to sit back and wait to be given information. The company is actively directing its efforts to alter the approach to information of this latter group.

Senior representatives in Company E also identified two distinct user groups. One senior manager described the differences in the groups as follows:

> There are probably two categories of users in a sense: those who are relatively new to it; and then the so-called 'power users' who are experienced in accessing the information warehouse or repository that is available them. So we have to recognize what category of user we are dealing with. The power user might well want something completely different. They don't just want their question answered, they probably want something about the information-gathering, or structuring process changing. So, you have to look at different issues with them, than you would with the person who's relatively new to the company and not entirely aware of the information resources available to them.

Senior staff in Company C can identify an information ethos in themselves; however, they believe this does not run through the organization as a whole. They describe a one-way flow of information in the organization, with a failure of communication from less senior staff members. The director of information systems offered an explanation for this observation:

> In terms of information about what's happening in the company, from a top-down perspective it is particularly good. I think the other way round, bottom-up, the workers informing the management of things, that's not so good. This is because of the changes going on in the industry at the moment. The people in the operational areas and the production areas know that the way things have happened in the past are not going to continue. The main reason for that is technology; where you would have an outside broadcast crew of seven or eight people, now you've got two or even one. Those changes are making life very difficult, so in terms of general information this goes one way, but for very understandable reasons it's not being reciprocated.

Representatives from the remaining companies surveyed either failed to identify a definite information ethos in their organizations, or identified problems which prevented the development of effective information policy. The experiences of Company G illustrate this latter point. Senior managers in Company G believe their problems arise from a lack of knowledge among staff members of the information resources that are available to them. One senior manager commented:

> There is an awful lot of key information in the company that people are not aware could be made available to them. For example, I give something like this [holds up a chart] to the store operations director and he thinks it's wonderful information and asks 'how did you get this?' We need to give people information and allow them to choose the value of it, and decide if they want to invest in that type of information in the future.

However, the company is attempting to improve the knowledge of their staff. A representative explained why:

> People don't realize what information is available or, even though it may be important, they don't bother asking for it. Or because they haven't had the information in front of them, or someone hasn't given them the information, it hasn't been identified as important information. It's just that kind of information-mining concept that is of potential value, and it's something we're starting to espouse through a lot of the business areas.

The education process has been initiated and supported by the company's chief executive. His contribution was described by a senior manager:

> I suppose one of our biggest advantages is that our chief executive is very switched on to the value of information... I believe our chief executive is in effect promoting the more effective use of information throughout the company and that's obviously helping.

A senior representative from Company H could not identify an effective information ethos, or information culture, in the organization. He commented:

> I don't think the value of information in itself is conveyed. Half the time it's not understood by the majority; the value of information is only understood when it's missing. It's taken as being there and probably not appreciated as such.

It's when you can't get hold of it that it becomes an issue.

Senior managers in companies F, I, J and K could not identify an information ethos in their organizations. A senior representative in Company J commented:

> With general information, well there's certainly a feeling it's everybody's company.

However, he was reluctant to describe this as an information ethos or culture in the company. A representative in Company K commented:

> The company's ethos encourages people to see information and IT as tools, which they need to do their work.

Representatives in Company I could not identify an information ethos in the company, and they admitted this was a problem. One senior representative stated:

> I don't think information is conveyed very well at the moment. I think that's a problem; it's actually not done very well.

The director of information systems in Company F described the company's attitude towards information dissemination as follows:

> Information is conveyed on a need-to-know basis. You won't necessarily disseminate all information... It is very much determined by what you need for your particular work.

Therefore, it is clear that over half the companies surveyed recognize the importance of information and are taking steps to create an information culture, or an information ethos, in their organizations. Of the rest, the majority have recognized the need to adopt a similar approach.

Conclusions

This research has highlighted some important issues that companies now face in the modern business environment. The recent mass introduction of information technology has confused the issues of information management and information provision. In the majority of the companies surveyed the traditional information specialist is playing a diminishing role in information provision. The role is being taken over by IT personnel who put the emphasis on effective storage and retrieval of information, rather than the quality of the information itself.

However, many of the senior staff in the more successful companies are now recognizing the importance of information management issues. The view that information is a valuable asset is almost universally accepted by the companies surveyed. Top management commitment to information as an asset has emerged as a major factor in the implementation of successful information systems.

The research has also highlighted the emphasis many companies put on internally-generated information. One reason for this may be that the companies surveyed are high performing in their sector and they therefore expect other companies to follow their example, and do not feel the need to invest time and effort investigating their competitors' actions.

The conclusions reached under each of the variables measured are listed below.

Technology

- The majority of companies surveyed see IT as essential to their business.
- IT and IS have been developed with the IT or IS departments working closely with the business functions.
- Companies have emphasized the importance of balance between involvement of user departments and technical IS or IT functions in the design of information systems.
- The majority of companies surveyed have benefited from top management commitment to IT and information in general.
- IS development in the more successful companies has been led

by the CEO.
- On the whole, company libraries have been slow to embrace new technology and new information roles.

Company knowledge base

- All the companies surveyed felt their knowledge base relied more on individuals than on systems.
- All the companies acknowledged the problems associated with having a knowledge base which relies too heavily on individuals rather than on systems.
- The need to conform to industry regulations along with the sensitivity of staff and customers has prevented some companies from introducing recent IT developments for information systems, or at least is advanced as an excuse for failing to do so.
- Company libraries are underfunded and understaffed and are therefore reluctant to take on a larger role in the organizations.
- Company libraries are perceived as service departments sitting on the fringe of the organizations.

Information sensitivity

- Senior staff in the more successful companies surveyed are acknowledging information management issues.
- Most of the companies surveyed circulate information on a regular basis. However, the major part of this is generated internally.
- An increasing number of companies are using information technology to support their information gathering and dissemination processes.
- A number of the companies surveyed hold information at too high a level within their organizations and fail to disseminate it effectively

Information ethos

- Information is seen as a valuable asset by the majority of the companies surveyed.
- The creation of an information ethos or culture is seen as an important step towards ensuring continued success by the

majority of the companies surveyed.
- The creation of an information ethos is part of an ongoing process of change management in some companies, partly initiated by the widespread introduction of information technology into the workplace.
- Those companies which have successfully implemented change and created an information ethos have done so with the backing and leadership of senior managers and the CEO in particular.

The research model

The research proved the legitimacy of the research model and validated the interconnected variables studied in the model. However, in the course of the research other important variables were identified. The original research model has been expanded to include environmental factors and internal organizational factors, both of which can influence business success and the implementation of successful information systems (Figure 6).

The expanded research model shows the following additional variables which have been identified in this study:

- The state of the market
- The nature of the industry
- Changes in legislation/government regulations
- Changes in the nature of competition
- Internal political turbulence
- The CEO's information ethos

The first four factors are external to the company and can have a profound impact on its internal structure and on its business success. The companies surveyed have identified these as factors which have prevented them from fully implementing successful information systems.

The fifth factor describes the reluctance of certain key staff members to embrace the creation of an information ethos and the introduction of IT into the organization.

The sixth factor is the information ethos of the Chief Executive Officer which has been identified as important by all the companies surveyed in ensuring the implementation of effective information systems. It was recognized by all the companies surveyed that the CEO is the one member of the organization with the power to initiate a process of change that is required in order to foster an information culture or ethos in the organization.

Figure 6: *The expanded research model*

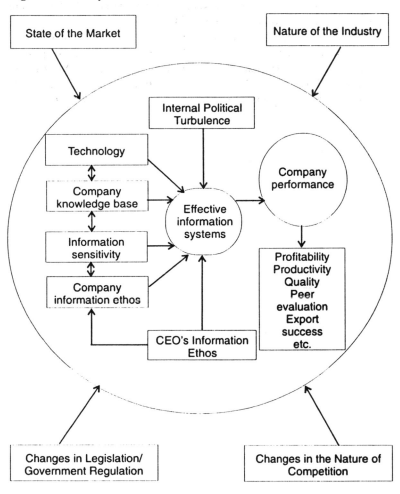

Recommendations for further research

It is clear that this is an area which requires more research. This project focused on high performing companies operating in different industries. A follow-up project could use the expanded research model to investigate information systems in less successful companies, although securing their cooperation may prove very difficult.

It would also be useful to focus on companies operating in a single industry, using the same research tools. In this way it would be possible to collect data on the variables identified in the expanded research model. These could then be used to test the validity of the expanded research model by comparing companies that face the same external influences.

References

Abell, A. and Winterman, V., (1992) *Information culture and business performance.* British Library Research and Development Department. December 1992.

Adler, P.S. (1989) Technology strategy: a guide to the literature. In *Research on Technological Innovation, Management and Policy,* ed. R.S. Rosenbloom and R.A. Burgleman, pp. 25-151. Greenwich, CT: JAI Press.

Bakos, Y. (1991) A strategic analysis of electronic marketplaces. *MIS Quarterly,* September, 295-312.

Banker, R.D. Kauffman, R.J. and Mahmood, M.A. (1993) Strategic information technology management: perspectives on organizational growth and competitive advantage. London.

Beer, M., Eisenstat, R.A. and Spector, B. (1990) *The critical path to corporate renewal.* Boston, MA: Harvard Business Press.

Bender, D. (1986) Financial impact of information processing. *Journal of Management Information Systems,* 3(2), 232-238.

Blair, J. (1986) An analysis of organizational productivity and the use of electronic information systems. *Proceedings of the 43rd Annual Meeting,* ASISS, pp. 236-238.

Cronin, B. and Gudmin, M. (1986) Information and productivity: a review of research. *International Journal of Information Management,* 6, 85-101.

DiNardo, G.P. and Williams, E.J. (1981) And now a word from 'big iron' bankers. *ABA Banking Journal,* May, 47-49.

Flowerdew, A.D.J. and Whitehead, C.M.E. (1974) *Cost effectiveness and cost benefit analysis in information science.* OSTL Report 5206. London: London School of Economics and Political Science.

Ginman, M. (1988) Information culture and business performance. *IATUL Quarterly,* 2(2), 93-106.

Harris, S.E. and Katz J.L. (1991) Firm size and the information technology investment intensity of life insurers. *MIS Quarterly,* 15, 333-352.

Herzog, O. (1994) Should we invest in intellectual elegance or computer power? *IFIP Transactions: Computer Science and Technologies*, n A **53**, 311-314.

Kettinger, W.J., Grover, V., Guha S. and Segars, A.H. (1994) Strategic information systems revisited: a study in sustainability and performance. *MIS Quarterly*, **18**(1), 31-58.

King, W.R. (1994) Forecasting productivity: the impact of IT. *Information Systems Management*, **11**(1), 68-70.

Koenig, M.E.D. (1982) *Research productivity and the information environment: a study within the pharmaceutical industry*. Rosary College, Illinois.

Kotter, J.P. (1982) *The General Manager*. New York: Free Press.

Loveman, G. (1988) An assessment of the productivity impact of information technologies. *Working Paper, Management in the 90s*. Sloan School of Management, MIT.

McFarlan, W.F. (1984) Information technology changes the way you compete. *Harvard Business Review*, May-June.

Markus, M.L. and Bjorn-Anderson, N. (1986) Power over users: its exercise by systems professionals. *Communications of the Association of Computing Machinery*, **30**.

May, B.R. (1979) EFT and branch automation. *The Magazine of Bank Administration*, February, 42-44.

Olson, M.H. and Weill, P. (1989) Managing investment in information technology: mini case examples and implications. *MIS Quarterly*, **13**(1), 3-17.

Parsons, G. L. (1983) Information technology: a new competitive weapon. *Sloan Management review*, **25**(1), 3-13.

Porter, M. (1985) *Competitive Advantage*. New York, NY: The Free Press.

Porter, M. and Millar, V.E. (1985) How information gives you competitive advantage. *Harvard Business Review*, **63**(4), 149-160.

Roberts, N. and Clarke, D. (1988) Case studies in business information aquisition. *CRUS News*, **30**, 35-6.

Silk, D. (1988) Towards better information management. *International Journal of Information Management*, **8**, 167-177.

Segars, A.H. and Grover, V. (1994) Strategic group analysis: a methodological approach for exploring the industry level impact of information technology. OMEGA *International Journal of Management Science*, **22**(1), 13-34.

Saunders, J., Brown, M. and Laverick, S. (1992) Research notes on the best British companies; a peer evaluation of Britain's leading firms. *British Journal of Management*, **3**, 181-195.

Venkataraman, N. (1994) IT-enabled business transformation: from automation to business scope redefinition. *Sloan Management Review*, **35**(20), 73-89.

White, D.A. and Wilson, T.D. (1987) Business information needs and the online supplier: lessons from recent research. In *National Online Meeting: Proceedings*, New York, 5-7 May 1987, pp. 477-481.

Wilson, T.D. (1987) Information for business: the business of information. *ASLIB Proceedings*, **39**(10), 275-279.

SECTION 2
THE CASE STUDIES

Company A

Company profile

Company A is one of the biggest water service providers in the country. It has an average turnover of between £250 and £500 million per year, and employs in excess of 1,500 people. Previously part of the public sector, the company was privatized in 1986. Its main activities are based in the UK, but it does have 29 immediate subsidiary companies, some of which operate worldwide.

Success factors

Like all recently privatized water companies, Company A operates a virtual monopoly, which makes its success, and the measures used to define success, difficult to identify. The Government-appointed water regulator (OFWAT) uses an efficiency rating based on capital expenditure to rate the companies, also taking into account other factors such as size.

The company has developed its own success model, which takes total expenditures, capital and revenue, and measures them against total outputs. On the basis of this model the company believes it is the most successful water services company in the country.

Reasons for success

One reason for the company's success is its size; with over ten million customers it is one of the country's largest water service providers. Other factors include:

- *People.* Since privatization the company has brought in a new set of top managers. From the CEO down, senior management has set about developing an environment, or culture, that fosters creativity and change.

- *Innovation in engineering.* Innovative approaches to engineering problems have saved the company money and maintained a high level of customer service.
- *Excellence in information technology and information management.* This has produced real savings, as well as improving customer service. For example, a current project, which relies heavily on IT and is aimed at understanding leakage, has delayed the need for a new £600 million reservoir for ten years.

The company believes continued success will depend on further streamlining the business, and further developing a culture that is responsive to change. A major factor in this will be the successful management of information already held in information systems and a number of programmes designed to achieve this are underway.

Measures of success

The company believes quality of management, although difficult to measure, is essential to achieving success. Financial soundness is useful, as is the capacity to innovate. Quality of products and services, and strategic thinking were both rated as very useful.

The company uses two additional success measures: product quality and customer satisfaction. Of these, product quality is the more important. The company defines product quality as the delivered product, i.e. clean drinking water, mechanisms used to deliver this water, and the predictability of the service; in other words, when the customer turns on the tap, water will come out. The company is proud of the fact that since privatization it has not imposed a hosepipe ban on its customers. This is due in part to the success of a major engineering project, supported by complex computer systems, which were recently awarded a British Computer Society award for software.

Before privatization the company did not have a department dedicated to dealing with customers. Since 1986 customer relations has become a major part of the business, representing a major shift of emphasis. In order to deal with this it has brought on line a number of information systems dedicated to customer service, and now has a customer service department.

OFWAT also monitors levels of customer service, grading each of the water companies on a scale of five, ranging from very poor to very good.

Company A has consistently received a rating of 'very poor'. However, a new information system called CIS (Customer Information System) is now in operation, with the result that the company's rating has improved dramatically and it is now confident of a 'very good' rating by OFWAT.

Competitors

Company A could not name a main competitor, since it operates in a true monopoly. It prefers to think in terms of comparative, rather than competitive, measures of success. Therefore, when planning its information strategy, the company is looking for systems that will produce comparative advantage.

The company uses performance indicators to measure the success of systems and strategies, and compares the results with other companies in the industry. OFWAT also uses performance indicators and ranks the companies accordingly. One result is the recently introduced 'K' factor. OFWAT has announced an average 'K' factor for the industry of one per cent. This means, on average, water bills will not be allowed to rise above one per cent above inflation for the next five years. Company A expects to be awarded a negative 'K' factor, which means there will be little or no increase in water bills for the consumer.

Information technology and information systems

The company believes one major breakthrough is the creation of a culture which enables it successfully to implement information systems. The main reason for this is seen to be the corporate sponsorship of the information systems strategy. The CEO is regarded as the major driver of this strategy, and each corporate project is sponsored by a director. If a director is unwilling to sponsor a project, it is cancelled.

User involvement

The Management Systems Department (MSD) looks for real involvement from users in the design and implementation of information systems. Each new project involves a multi-disciplinary team of people, the balance of which will shift as the project progresses. For example:

- *feasibility*: four users to one IS professional
- *high level design*: balance shifts to two to one

- *development*: three to one
- *systems testing and implementation*: two to one

The user, or customer as the company prefers, is also involved heavily in the initial strategy phase. The reason for this is that the user is responsible for managing the implementation of the system, and managing the savings the system is designed to produce. The user is encouraged to take part fully in this process and, indeed, is made personally responsible for the savings, improved quality, improved performance, or whatever other improvements the system was designed to deliver. The company believes this level of involvement in the information systems development process differentiates it from other companies.

Information technology

Company A uses information technology to deliver information services in a number of ways. It has had an Executive Information System (EIS) for three years. This is available on the PC of every director, and has proved to be very effective. It now plans to broaden the scope and range of its EIS, to deliver a service to every senior manager. The company hopes to utilize emerging technologies to make EIS part of its every day business.

On the other hand, it has made limited use of expert systems. These systems are described as 'very expert mathematical models', rather than expert systems and the company rated them as effective.

E-mail is used extensively for internal communication, and has been found to be very effective. E-mail is now the common denominator for information flow within the company.

Automatic ordering and supply systems are also described as being very effective. The company has recently started a pilot programme for Electronic Data Interchange (EDI) which it believes will be very effective, although it is too early to rate its success.

The company's information systems enable it to monitor a number of variables. It monitors its own performance effectively, but believes it is not very effective at monitoring the performance of other similar water companies. When asked to rate the information systems' effectiveness in monitoring general changes in the market the company assumed a neutral position. The company believes it is very effective in monitoring other internal variables, including product quality, delivery performance, compliance and leakage.

Information strategy

The company does not have an IT strategy group. The information strategy is owned by the CEO and the board, and is the vehicle used to define the scope, objectives, costs and priorities for information systems. The current information strategy was developed between 1986 and 1989 in an interactive process between the board and the users, and has been implemented during the last four years.

An important aspect of the strategy is that it is designed to support business processes, rather than individual departments. Departments within the company are organized vertically, while business processes tend to be defined horizontally. If information systems are to support the business processes they must move horizontally across the business. Therefore, the information strategy had to be organizationally independent and driven by the CEO and the board.

The next stage in this process is to utilize the information from the systems to change the way the business is managed, to re-engineer business processes so that they use this information to best effect. The MSD is currently embarked on such a project. One example is the procurement process. Three years ago the company had 25 warehouses, £17 million worth of stock, 80 depots and 1,800 employees. This process has been re-engineered, and today the company has one warehouse, £6 million worth of stock and 20 depots, and has cut the workforce by 350.

Evaluating information systems

The company evaluates the effectiveness of its information systems in two ways: bottom line impact and performance. Bottom line impact describes the effect of the system on the function it is designed to support. The finance department discusses the expected financial impact of the system with the managers in the areas concerned, and they change the business plan accordingly. The system's impact on the business plan is then monitored closely.

Performance-related variables are also monitored closely. These are quantitative, activity related impacts of the system on the business. For example: is the process now more effective in terms of costs and time? These variables are quantified and measured.

Company A regards its information systems as vital to its business. Now the systems infrastructure is in place the company believes it is reaping the benefits—major cost savings and quality enhancements that are moving it towards becoming one of the best companies in Britain.

The company knowledge base

Company A considers itself to be information intensive, rather than knowledge intensive. Increasingly, information is held in systems. This can be contrasted with the way the company operated before privatization. Then the company depended heavily on individuals' knowledge and expertise; it operated very much in a empirical way, based on a combination of rule sets and local knowledge. Much of this information is now contained in a comprehensive Geographic Information System (GIS). This is a full client server system that contains every element of the company's water distribution network. This information is available in every depot, and to every inspector's desktop. The GIS monitors constantly the flow of water through the water network.

The company's information systems have created a huge repository of data; the problem it now faces is how to utilize this information. To solve this problem the company has initiated a project designed to ask managers two fundamental questions:

- What information do you need to run your business?
- How do I get you that information?

The results of this project will be used to provide a Business Information Service (BIS), to replace the limited EIS now in use. It is hoped that the BIS will become fundamental to the way managers do their business. Much of this information is held in mainframe SKADA and ICA systems. The company has developed an Operational Management System (OMS) to compile information from the mainframe into a relational database that will be accessible on a desktop PC. The MSD has developed a series of decision support and reporting systems which, together with modelling tools, will enable individual managers to manipulate the data.

Information resources

A library is situated in head office which grew out of a function that supported scientists working in the company. This library now provides support to other functions, including management systems, computer support, management functions, emergency planning, as well as operational departments. A second library supports the engineering functions. Some other departments have their own collections of reference materials but these are not organized as a library. The main library has a number of information resources at its disposal, including over 120 journal subscriptions and a number of CD-ROM subscriptions. The CD-ROMs include *Aqualine, EC Infodisc, Bookfind, Best,* and the American Water Works Association's *Water Net.*

The most regular users of the library are the environmental group, the water biologists, emergency planning, and the finance department. The library has online access through Dialplus to Dialog, Datastar, Dialtech, Blaise, Reuters, Textline, and Orbit online databases.

The library also has its own database management system, which has been online since early 1995 and is available on the company's computer network. The selection of the software and the design of the database management system was undertaken as a collaboration between the library and the information systems department. The company librarian had the final say, and other library staff were consulted in the selection process.

The information the library collects reflects the company's varied business interests. For example, the most repeated searches are for company information, ranging from simple searches for telephone numbers, to searches for financial data on companies, and complete company profiles. The library also conducts searches for specialist scientific information, and for information specific to the water industry.

Library staff make no effort to advertise their services within the company. This is because they feel the library has been under-funded and undermanned in recent years, so that the amount of work they do at the moment already exceeds their resources. However, the new management database does advertise the service since it is accessible online by most staff members. The library also produces two current awareness bulletins each year, which go some way towards raising the profile of the library in the company, as well as circulating a limited number of periodicals to departments within the company, and ordering additional books and journals when staff make a formal request.

The library does provide some training in information skills to the company, although this is limited due to a lack of resources. Staff feel they could provide more in the way of training if more resources were available. The information provided by the library to the company is seen as a valuable resource. In the past this information has been used to create new business opportunities and to help the decision makers formulate strategies for future development. Staff feel they could do more, but a lack of money and trained personnel prevents them from doing so.

Knowledge transfer

Individuals' knowledge and expertise are communicated to other members of staff in a very traditional way. Most communication is either formal, in meetings, or informal, by talking to people in the company. This traditional method of communication is gradually changing, and the company is embarked on a programme with the aim of understanding processes and building rule sets so knowledge can be, to a limited degree, systematized. Two important aspects of this are constructing models, or rule sets, and collecting accurate data to run the models. The process involves information systems professionals sitting down with staff to encapsulate the rule sets that they have, and link this to the data contained in systems.

Information transfer

Internal information is communicated electronically, via the company's e-mail system. External information is generated by three departments in the company. The Public Relations department produces a press cuttings service, while another department looks at environmental issues that affect the company. Information from both departments is summarized and passed through the e-mail system. A third department carries out comparative studies, comparing the company with other companies in the industry. This department produces 'Key Facts and Comparative Indicators', which is circulated monthly on a floppy disc.

Problems locating information

There are some problems locating information once it is inside the company. However, three years ago the company introduced a corporate policy on records management, and now puts a lot of effort into indexing information in systems.

The company is also developing active work flow systems which are designed to integrate structured data with paper images. A pilot system, linking images of letters with existing customer data, has been set up in the Customer Services Department which receives over one million letters each year. The company believes this system will be of great benefit to the business.

Information ethos

The company is working very hard to create a culture that encourages awareness of information. They are also attempting to introduce the concept of information management into the company. The information systems strategy, for example, is now called the information strategy. This process is not without its problems. However, the company is making an effort. It is moving away from simply developing information systems towards looking at information itself, relating information to the business and using that information to make decisions.

Information and business objectives

Company A has three key business objectives: to produce excellent product quality; to excel in customer service; and to remain very cost-effective, with the lowest combined water and sewerage bill in the country. The company's information systems and services have been designed so as to help meet these objectives and its information ethos has been an important part of this process.

Training and human resources

The process of creating an information culture has involved considerable effort in developing staff's information and IT skills. With every major information systems project that is put in place, 40 per cent of the budget is spent on 'change management', which is essentially about education and training. When projects have, in the past, failed to deliver the savings that were expected, the company found it was due to lack of training.

The company now appoints a 'product manager' to take total responsibility for the administration of a new information system, including system support and maintenance, data integrity, systems administration, and user education and training. This has proved to be effective, in terms of both saving money, and effectively managing the implementation of user systems on a continuous basis. The company also develops computer-based training tools to support new applications. These are available to staff both online and in off-line training rooms.

The company feels that all staff members are generally aware of all the information resources that are available to them, although they concede that there is still a long way to go before all staff are happy using them.

Company B

Company profile

Company B is a medium-sized UK based building society. It has assets totalling £25,000 million, with 4.5 million investment accounts and 549,000 mortgage borrowers. The company has a network of retail branches and estate agencies throughout the UK and Europe, and employs over 8,000 staff. In 1993 the company made a pre-tax profit of £217 million and had a cost-to-income ratio of 49.3.

Success factors

Company B considers itself to be very successful and believes it outperforms the bulk of its competitors. When compared with other financial service providers, the company is successful in terms of traditional financial yardsticks: asset growth, profitability and annual turnover.

Reasons for success

The company believes three factors contribute to its success:

- a traditionally conservative, low risk-taking approach to business
- good standing with the customers in the market place
- a broad range of products provided to personal customers

These factors reflect the company's style and are part of a long established and successful formula. It may not take every business opportunity that presents itself, but avoids making mistakes. As a building society company B believes that it has an inherently friendlier image than banks; it also believes it has a reputation for fairness, value and service. Through its extensive branch network, the company is able to provide a broad range of financial services to the personal customer, as opposed to corporate or small business customers.

The traditional core business of the building society is savings and mortgage lending. Since the 1986 deregulation of the financial services industry the company has diversified into estate agency, property development, unit trusts and life insurance, and is now able to provide multiple products and services to the same customer. This diversification has benefited the company in two ways: it can provide customers with all their financial service requirements so that they need not go elsewhere, thus developing customer loyalty; and, because of its branch network, it can do without separate sales forces and delivery channels, thereby generating economies of scale and cutting costs.

Measures of success

The company considers financial soundness to be a very useful measure of success and important in helping to underpin its reputation with its customers. Quality of management is also considered useful, but not the most useful measure of success.

The quality of products and services is rated as neutral when considering success, largely because the quality of financial services does not really vary in the industry. A mortgage is a mortgage—it enables the customer to buy a house. What differentiates companies is the quality of the service to customers, rather than the quality of the product, and the company sees this as a very useful measure.

The capacity to innovate is also considered neutral as a measure of success. This would have been rated differently five years ago when the industry was deregulated. However, since then the company has been through a process of diversification, and feels it is unlikely to experience any further changes. Innovation at product level is also considered to be of little importance. This is regarded as more of a tactical game, striving for marginal advantage by catching the customer's attention.

The ability to think strategically is considered extremely important in achieving success. Export success is relevant to the company; it does not export any tangible goods, but does export its products and services. As a result of the diversification process the company now has operating subsidiaries in Northern Italy and France, with off-shore investment operations based in Guernsey, and agencies in Dubai and Hong Kong. This geographic diversification has proved useful in a number of ways, including helping to minimize the cyclical effects of the UK economy on the business. For example, the Guernsey operation has taken more retail investment than the whole of the UK operation in the last year due to UK market conditions.

The company considers environmental responsibility to be useful to success. It has a broad range of measures to reinforce its environmentally friendly image with the public, such as the corporate sponsorship of appropriate environmental events.

Financial performance is seen as a more appropriate measure than financial soundness. Financial soundness is associated with asset strength and capital adequacy regulations, whereas financial performance describes profitability and maintaining the appropriate cost-to-income ratios. The latter are considered important, dynamic factors and are measured continually. The company has a very substantial management accounting function which is able to generate profitability analysis down to individual branch level.

Comparative measures, such as the annual Union of Building Societies ratings and monthly market share statistics, are seen as a useful check on the company's performance against its own targets and objectives.

Competitors

The company has a large number of competitors, which fall into two groups, direct and niche competitors.

Direct competitors are other building societies and banks that offer the same financial services to the same customer group. In terms of products, services and size, the company has about five main competitors.

Since 1986 the financial service industry has allowed previously separate sectors to compete with each other. This has led to a growth in the number of niche competitors that compete with company B in a limited way, including large insurance companies, unit trust companies, and high street retailers and supermarket chains. For example, several supermarket chains now offer their customers a facility called 'cash back', which competes directly with company B's ATM (Automatic Teller Machine) network. The company takes this threat seriously.

The company's information systems monitor various aspects of the market. Those that monitor its own performance are regarded as effective. There is room for improvement, though, and the company is currently going through a process designed to update these systems.

The systems that provide competitor information are effective overall in monitoring main competitors, but not in monitoring the niche competitors that have emerged over the last few years, and the company feels that it needs to devote more resources to this area. In terms of monitoring changes in general market conditions, the company feels this is done very effectively, not because the company has invested a great deal of money in developing systems, but because the sources are relatively numerous and freely available. For example, two of the company's main competitors publish quarterly house price surveys that company B uses as an information source. It also buys information on market statistics from HMSO and subscribes to a number of online sources of market information. This information is fed into a dynamic econometric model that is then used to predict the effects of swings in the market.

The company considers it important to monitor two additional variables. Changes, or potential changes, in government policy that will influence the economy, and thus the marketplace, are closely monitored. The company also has systems in place that provide it with information and intelligence on changes in the financial services regulatory framework so that it can take advantage of these, or avoid any negative effects they might have on the business. For example, the regulatory body has announced that from 1 January 1995 life insurance commission will have to be disclosed to the customer. The likely impact of this is that life insurers will shift their pricing policy. Instead of front-loading the commission on to the earlier premiums in the policy, the insurer will probably add the administration costs later in the policy.

Information technology and information systems

The company makes extensive use of information technology but its current information systems put it at a significant disadvantage in relation to its key competitors. The company's corporate strategy is to achieve low cost production, but a number of its mainstream systems are not cost-effective, partly because it is operating 'legacy systems' that were written in the 1970s. In order to bring the cost base down, the legacy systems that drive the company's core businesses—mortgage lending, investment savings and banking—will be replaced over the next four years with modern systems and cost-effective information solutions to bring the company into line with its main competitors.

User involvement

Over a period of five years the company has made efforts to ensure the direct involvement of users, both management and staff, in every stage of the systems development process and believes this transition is one of the best policies it has ever implemented. The primary driver has been the introduction of the concept of 'value chain analysis', a customer-oriented approach to service provision. The Information Services department see themselves as providing a service to internal customers, who in turn use it to deliver a service to external customers. Each link in this chain provides added value, in order to maximize the service to the final customers.

Users now specify the design for input/output screens, specify the information to be contained in reports, and do all the system testing. Increasingly, they are developing their own systems, using modern application development tools such as screen painters and code generators. In this way those people who understand the business processes, or really understand the information needs of the business, now have the biggest say in the system development process.

The user is also involved in the delivery of information and computer services. End-user staff and management are actively involved in negotiating service-level agreements, so, for example, they can make sure that systems are available for the hours necessary to support the business, rather than the hours that are convenient to the IS department.

Information technology

Company B has experimented with the application of expert systems in a number of business processes, although the results have been disappointing. The problem was less to do with the technology than with the staff and customers who have failed to accept the technology. There have also been difficulties in meeting compliance regulations, perhaps because the encapsulation of expertise within a system is beyond their scope.

The company has a well established Executive Information System (EIS), which is delivered to the desktop of every executive from the Managing Director down. The EIS is PC-based and mouse-driven, and displays key performance information graphically, with exception analysis and other features. The system provides performance information across the business, from corporate level to individual branches. The company considers this system to be very effective.

The company makes extensive use of e-mail, and considers it to be very effective. Every staff member has access to e-mail and it is widely used to the extent that, over the last five years, it has largely replaced paper as the common medium for internal communication. One result has been the introduction of a diary or calendar management online system: all staff diaries are now online, which saves not only time scheduling meetings, but also money, by freeing staff to do other work.

The company makes limited use of EDI systems, but where they are used they are judged effective. A telebanking solution is being developed, which will make some use of voice recognition technology. Although not yet in place, the company believes it will be very effective. Videoconferencing is limited to communicating with European subsidiaries, but is considered effective.

Information strategy

The Information Systems Strategy (ISS) is produced and documented by the Information Systems (IS) department in three volumes. The first describes the resource and financial plans and is basically a high level work programme. The second volume forms the basis of the company's business process re-engineering and describes how the business processes are translated into target systems architecture—the appropriate systems and applications needed to run the business.

The third volume is an IT strategy document and specifies the technical directions, standards and protocols for all aspects of the technological base. In other words, it describes how the component technical parts of the information systems are put together and integrated effectively, providing a decision framework for individual project designs and information solutions.

The ISS is a dynamic document which is reviewed and republished annually as part of the corporate planning and budget planning review. It is thus implicitly related to the corporate and business strategies.

The IS department is also responsible for monitoring the business in order to identify any processes that might benefit from an improved information solution. For example, if the company decides to open up a new business in Europe, senior staff from the IS department will be involved in the formative stage of the business plan in order to ensure the IT component is properly worked in and supported. If any business opportunity derives directly from a technological advance the IS department actively seeks involvement to pursue that opportunity.

All hardware and software requirements are met through a central IT function and the company believes this benefits the business in a number of ways. All software used in the company is uniform across business functions. This means that the training department does not have to provide support for a number of different applications, avoiding the costs of diversity. By organizing a service around a critical mass usage, the company benefits from economies of scale.

Evaluating information systems

The company evaluates both the operational performance and the business effectiveness of its information systems but believes the evaluation process could be improved.

The company believes it is very good at evaluating the operational performance of information systems; service level agreements are in place to monitor the reliability of the system. It is less effective in evaluating the functional performance, or business effectiveness, of systems. However, since it intends to replace many of its core systems over the next few years this is not seen as a problem. The company has decided to allocate resources to building new systems rather than looking at short term opportunities of making current systems more effective.

The replacement systems will be designed and built to support business processes effectively at the time they are implemented and to monitor operational performance. However, mechanisms designed to evaluate business effectiveness may be left out.

The company knowledge base

The company considers itself to be information intensive. However, this response needs careful consideration. Information within information systems is judged essential to business operations; indeed, information processing is a fundamental part of the financial service sector. However, the company is keen to point out that information systems support rather than drive the business. In other words, information systems are seen as a tool to support management and staff in the execution of the business. Because the business is largely decentralized to the point of sale, staff need extensive knowledge of products and business processes. The company believes the expert knowledge of staff cannot be encapsulated within information systems.

Information resources

The company has a corporate information centre, situated in the corporate planning department, which operates as a specialist library designed to meet the needs of the company. It is not extensive, in the sense of an academic library, but focuses on particular activities of the company and knowledge of the markets the company is involved in. Its holdings include journals on the financial industry, particularly in the areas of mortgage lending, estate agency, economics and banking, along with economic statistics, financial statistics, economic indicators, and statistical analysis materials. The centre is responsible for supporting the management information systems, as well as the marketing and European development functions, and subscribes to journals and collects statistical material to meet these requirements.

The corporate planning department makes the most regular use of the information centre, followed by marketing and the company executive. Other departments also collect information resources that may be relevant to their work and store these locally. However, these do not constitute an organized collection.

The centre makes some use of information technology. It has access to the *FT Profile* online database, and conducts searches for departments on request. The centre is also responsible for the distribution of management information. This is generated internally by the operational units, fed into a large database, manipulated within the database using modelling tools, and then made available to the executive and senior managers via the company's online EIS. The system deals primarily with internal information, but does include a small amount of external information such as economic indicators, housing market indicators, and other subsidiary information. There is also a facility for merging data on the company's performance with similar data from the building society's association, so that the company's market share can be calculated.

The information centre staff were fully involved in the selection and design of the systems they use. This process involved the corporate planning department, which defined the system requirements, working in partnership with the technical division to come up with the right technical solutions to meet those requirements. The system was developed in-house, with some elements of commercial software included in the final package, and was implemented by the corporate planning department.

The information centre does not formally advertise itself within the company, relying on word of mouth communication to ensure staff are aware of the services it offers. It does not provide any formal training in information skills to the company. Staff within the company's head office are aware of the services the centre provides, whereas staff in different parts of the organization, for example the branch network, are unlikely to make any use of its facilities. The centre is more a resource for the decision makers, who value the information it provides in a number of ways: it provides a lot of information relating to market share analysis; its resources also help the top management to form effective corporate strategies.

Knowledge transfer

The expert knowledge of individuals within the company is communicated to other members of staff in three ways. Firstly, although the e-mail system is used extensively to communicate information, the company relies more on the traditional hierarchical structure of the organization for vertical knowledge transfer. There is a hierarchy of supervisory managers, for example branch managers and assistant branch managers, whose role is to train, develop and pass knowledge to their staff.

Secondly, the company has a strong commitment to train and develop all staff. It was one of the first to win the 'Investors in People' award, and has established a comprehensive personal development programme for all staff.

Thirdly, the company relies heavily on substantial documentation of procedures and product knowledge. There is a control framework that supports the dissemination of knowledge through the business. This information is maintained in paper form, but the company plans to make it available online in a hypertext application.

Information transfer

Information is circulated to departments on a continuous basis. The common medium for the communication of internal information is the e-mail system, featuring a bulletin board, which is accessible by all staff and is used to advertise general company information, such as job vacancies, changes in organizational structure and new appointments. Internal mechanisms are mostly system supported. The company also circulates a lot of paper documents, but the amount of paper will reduce as more and more information is made available online.

External information is largely available on paper, although the company does subscribe to a number of CD-ROM titles and some online information services. Information about journal articles is circulated on paper. External information is also communicated through formal and informal meetings, conferences and seminars. For example, every six months the heads of the information services of the top fifteen building societies meet to discuss issues facing the industry. This process is seen as a very effective method of communicating information.

Problems locating information

The company experiences some problems in this area, but these are not considered significant. The company recognizes the best horizontal flow of information is at a fairly senior level and this may lead to local objectives being out of line with corporate objectives. Another problem can arise if new projects are not fully understood by line managers because horizontal communication has been inadequate.

Information ethos

The company clearly recognizes the value of information, and understands that it should maximize this value by making it available to all those within the company who can benefit from it. However, there is a less than systematic approach to the distribution of information. Some information is held at too senior a level. In order to rectify this the company is working on the devolution of decision-making responsibility, or 'flattening' the organizational structure. Progress is being made, but is slow.

The company believes it has the right attitude, but progress is hindered because some parts are operating under a management style that is less than facultative. Some managers consider information is power and act as a barrier to the free flow of information. The company believes it going through a learning process, and part of this involves teaching managers that their purpose is to encourage the effectiveness of the people who do the work.

Information and business objectives

The company's business objectives can be summarized as:

- maintaining profitable financial strength
- the sustained delivery of effective customer service
- sustained growth
- ensuring the effective and satisfying employment of staff

The company considers its information systems are designed to achieve these business objectives. They concede that as a result of the legacy of some previous decisions this alignment is not 100 per cent complete, but the strategic plan and systems development work plan are designed to meet this target.

Training and human resources

The company makes considerable effort to train all staff in IT and information skills and its personal development plan is designed to improve staff competence, skills, knowledge and business awareness.

To support the development process the company has an open learning centre with a number of PC-based training applications, CD-ROMs, and interactive video services on a whole range of topics, from effective correspondence to an advanced tutorial on spreadsheets. There is also a residential centre that provides management development training.

The company also provides sponsorship for staff to participate in external education courses. It has its own Business Studies degree programme and a Diploma in Management. Staff are encouraged to take National Vocational Qualifications to develop their skills and further broaden their knowledge. Training programmes are complemented by specific work context objectives which enable staff to apply their training.

Additional effort has to be applied before all staff are aware of the information resources that are available to them. Attitudes towards information and knowledge transfer vary across the organization. In general, the company feels too much information stays high in the organizational hierarchy, and there is not enough horizontal movement of information.

Company C

Company profile

Company C is a regional independent television provider with an annual turnover of over £2,000 million and over 30,000 employees. When compared with the industry as a whole the company has a return on capital in the upper quartile range.

Company C has been recently acquired by a larger regional television company. The new grouping is now the largest company in the Independent Television (ITV) network, commanding a third of all ITV revenue, and is the second largest single supplier of programmes to this network.

Success factors

The company sees itself as one of the more successful companies in the ITV network, in terms of both the quality of its programmes and its share of advertising revenue.

Reasons for success

The company believes there are several factors that contribute to its success. It has some very talented people on the programme-making side of the business, and it also spends a lot of time promoting its schedule. The company feels it is particularly good at this aspect of the business.

It has also rationalized its business, halving its workforce in the last two years, and has been at the forefront of changing the way people work in the industry. The changes have been made in both the operational and production areas of the business, enabling the company to become more cost-effective.

Measures of success

The company uses a number of success measures, including quality of management, financial soundness, capacity to innovate, and ability to think strategically. The quality of products and services was judged very useful, indeed essential, to the success of the company. Export success and environmental responsibility were not considered of any particular importance.

The primary success measure is audience share, which is the one thing that all television companies measure their success against. A one per cent increase in audience share can add millions of pounds to the company's profit, so other success measures tend to pale into insignificance. The company monitors this on a daily basis.

Competitors

All other television companies are seen as competitors. The recent changes in the way independent television is organized has caused some confusion in the industry. The company's main competitor was considered to be the company that has recently acquired it. Cable and satellite television also represent a growing threat. The company believes that terrestrial television companies will start to lose their market share as cable and satellite establish themselves in the country. If it is to enjoy continued success, the company will have to increase its share of a decreasing market.

Information technology and information systems

The company believes it has more effective information systems than many of its rivals. Indeed, it draws attention to the fact that it developed the systems now run by a number of companies in the ITV network. Every process in the company is now supported by information systems.

User involvement

The company wants the end user to be the primary driver of the information strategy. It believes in the near future there will no longer be a need for a specific information systems department. Rather, end users will develop their own applications using modern application development tools.

Information strategy

The company produces an annual information strategy document based on its three year plan. The three year plan is usually updated every year. However, in the last few years changes in the industry structure have thrown this into disarray.

The information strategy has been based each year on what senior managers within the company see themselves requiring over the next twelve months. Because this is not linked with any corporate plan it cannot be described as truly strategic. During this period the company has not invested in any large scale systems development. Instead, it has spent the last three years developing an information infrastructure intended to meet the future information needs of the company. This is reflected in the move towards more end user involvement in the information systems development process.

The information infrastructure is also intended to help re-engineer the business processes to gain advantage from the systems that are already in place. One example of this is the system that supports the scheduling process. The schedule is made up of the programmes, commercials, promotion values and presentation elements. The schedule planning process starts eighteen months in advance, and is refined until the company has an actual transmission schedule which is then passed to automatic transmission equipment. A pilot scheme was introduced in this area which illustrated that the process could be made more efficient by reorganizing the department, using technology to change what people do. It is important to point out that this exercise was driven by business rather than technology; technology was used to redefine the process from a business perspective. The company now wishes to apply this methodology to the rest of the business.

Evaluating information systems

Every two or three years all systems are assessed to determine their effectiveness. All major systems have steering groups attached which meet every three months and discuss any enhancements that need to be made. In 1993 the company's information systems were assessed by external consultants who gave them a clean bill of health. The information systems are assessed continually and, in general, the company believes they are very effective.

The company knowledge base

The company considers itself to be information intensive. Indeed, as a media company, its main role is processing and presenting information—news, sport and regional information. The company has three departments dedicated to collecting and storing information: the press office, stills library and film library.

The company libraries make limited use of information systems. Improving the information services in the libraries is one area which the company plans to look at in the future. At the moment the company relies on the librarians to use their knowledge to collect and maintain reference materials. The company also has access to other, external libraries, and some departments subscribe to online information services provided by the Press Association and Reuters.

Information resources

The company's reference/stills library provides information resources and still photographs to programme makers. In addition to still photographs it has a collection of reference materials—books, encyclopaedias, dictionaries and periodicals. The library also keeps newspapers on file, mostly for six months, but in some cases for up to two years. There is no cuttings service, but it does make use of an online database to provide a similar service. At the moment the library has no CD-ROM facilities, but there are plans to purchase a reader and subscribe to *Hansard* on CD.

The most regular users of the library are the programme makers. The company presently produces 29 news bulletins a day, and also makes a number of current affairs and documentary programmes. The library provides the information resources and all the reference materials for these, and the library staff act as researchers for the programme makers.

The press office makes some use of the library facilities, as does the community affairs unit. Other departments make occasional use of the resources in the library, but the main users are the programme makers.

The library's online database was designed by the library staff in cooperation with the Information Systems Department. It consists of a subject database, with indexed periodicals, books, newspaper articles and still photograph information. It is a free-text database and is commonly used to search for information on personalities who may be involved in the news. The library also subscribes to the *Financial Times*

Profile online database, and staff will search this to provide information to programme makers.

The library does not advertise its services, but relies on word of mouth. It is such an integral part of the programme-making procedure that it already has a high profile within the company. The library does not currently provide any training in information skills to departments within the company, but this may change if the library database is provided online to other departments. The library staff believe the information they provide enables the company to remain successful in a very competitive industry. Programmes cannot be made without the research and accurate information which the library provides.

Knowledge transfer

Expert knowledge within the company is not communicated effectively to other members of staff. In certain areas procedures and technical information are held in manuals, but most information is retained in people's heads.

The organizational changes in recent years have entailed a rationalization of the workforce, and this process is set to continue as the business of providing and supporting television production continues to change. In this climate, the company feels it would not be wise to attempt to extract information from its workforce, as any move to do so might be seen as an attempt to make some staff redundant. However, a lot of specific knowledge, especially technical knowledge, will soon be obsolete. The company therefore plans to implement the necessary organizational changes, invest in new broadcast technology, and then start to move information from people into electronic forms.

Information transfer

General internal information is communicated through the company effectively, mostly via an internal teletext television system that is available on screens in every office and in all communal areas.

Other information is communicated by paper. This includes daily and quarterly schedules and daily ratings, which are circulated to over one hundred managers in the company. External information is also circulated on paper, and the company has no plans to automate this. The company describes its process of disseminating information as a 'scatter gun approach', and believes it to be very effective.

Problems locating information

The company feels staff experience no real problems locating information once it is inside the company. One reason for this is the 'scatter gun' approach to dissemination; information is circulated to so many people within the company that few can have problems finding it.

Information ethos

As a media company, senior management are very aware of the need to communicate information effectively. This is done via notice boards, teletext and regular staff briefings. Managers at all levels are encouraged to hold regular briefings with their staff. The company feels that top-down communication within the company is very effective, but bottom-up communication—the workers informing the management—is not so good. The main reason for this is the suspicion among staff members that the organizational changes will cost them their jobs. This is especially true of the operational and production areas which have borne the brunt of the job cuts; in the past an outside broadcast crew would require seven or eight people, but new technology has cut this to two. Therefore, the company feels that while information is being communicated one way, for understandable reasons it is not being reciprocated.

Information and business objectives

The company's key business objectives may be summarized as:

- operate the regional ITV licence within ITC guidelines
- maximize air-time sales revenue
- maximize audience share
- produce quality programmes to be shown on the ITV network and sold overseas

The company information strategy concentrates on these areas and is therefore driven by the business objectives. In other words, systems that do not address these objectives should not be developed.

Training and human resources

The company puts considerable effort into training all staff members in IT and information skills. It feels very aware of this need; even when other budgets have been cut, money has been found for staff development. For example, when new hardware is bought the training department automatically provides training for staff in the software used by the system.

Sponsorship is provided for staff to take appropriate external courses. The company's management training course is comprehensive, covering all aspects of management, business finance and outward bound type courses. In addition to developing skills, these courses provide an opportunity for staff from different parts of the organization to meet informally.

The company considers that, in general, most staff are aware of most of the information resources available to them. It believes it has more knowledge than many other similar organizations, and is above average in communicating this information.

Company D

Company profile

Company D is a large, British-based food and dairy producer, specializing in short shelf-life products, biscuits, and milk production. The company generates annual sales in excess of £2,000 million, with an average turnover of over £1,000 million, and employs in excess of 10,000 people.

Success factors

The company is very successful in relation to the industry as a whole and its quartiles are in the upper range. It has performed well through the recent recession. In general, the food industry has been hit hard by the recession; the last twelve months have seen food price deflation for the first time in living memory. Another potential threat to the success of the industry, and to the company's continued success, is the deregulation of the milk industry with the abolition of the Milk Marketing Board.

Reasons for success

The company believes it owes its success to its partnership with food retailers which enables it to adapt its products to meet their needs. Its concentration on short shelf-life products means it has to be able to react quickly to new tastes and trends. The company therefore puts a lot of effort into product development and innovation. Linked to this is a policy of constantly changing products in order to offer a degree of choice to the customer.

Measures of success

Quality of management, financial soundness, quality of products and services, and the capacity to innovate are all considered very useful measures. Strategic thinking is rated useful, but the company considers environmental responsibility of no special importance. The company measures its success in terms of product quality, service and financial returns. Under the service banner the company includes innovation and the short lifecycle of products.

Competitors

The company has several competitors, the number varying in individual sectors. In each sector there is a small number of competitors of a similar size, along with some smaller companies which are quite successful.

The company has information systems that enable it effectively to monitor its own performance, assessing the performance of every company in the group on a weekly basis. It is also able to monitor changes in general market conditions but considers monitoring its main competitors' performance to be of neutral importance. Two other aspects of the market are considered to be important to the business: monitoring competitor innovation in product development; and monitoring competitors' financial performance.

Information technology and information systems

The company uses information technology to deliver information services in a number of ways, the extent to which they are used varying according to the sector concerned. In general, the company believes its use of information technology and the information systems it has in place enable it to keep one step ahead of most of its competitors.

User involvement

The company feels it involves users in the selection and the design of information systems. Most are either written in-house or chosen in-house by the users. The information systems department adopts an enabling role, allowing decisions to be made by the staff members who are going to use the systems.

Information technology

The company has an effective Executive Information System (EIS) and makes good use of electronic mail. Its automatic ordering and supply systems are very effective, as is its use of Electronic Data Interchange (EDI).

Hardware is supplied and serviced by a separate company. The company has used this computer supplier for a number of years, and has never found a good reason to change. The hardware platform has been cost effective to maintain. The company has evaluated the possibility of switching to other hardware platforms, but any savings would be minimal.

Information strategy

The company does not have a formal, written information systems strategy but endeavours to provide adequate support systems to enable staff to do their work. At the same time, it avoids being at the leading edge of information systems; in other words, it will invest only in tried and tested information systems solutions.

Another aspect of the company's attitude towards systems development is that all systems decisions are made at a local level, rather than being determined from the centre. This process is consolidated by a group reporting system which is conducted from the centre and interprets the local decisions. The company's strategy is designed to keep operating costs to a minimum, and to monitor all aspects of company performance. Company performance is monitored on a weekly basis.

Evaluating information systems

The company evaluates the effectiveness of its information systems on an informal basis, which involves looking at individual systems and measuring whether the actual benefits derived from the system match the forecasted benefits. The development processes are also assessed, and any difficulties that may have been experienced are noted. The company feels this process is rather too informal, and this is one area that will be examined in the future.

The company knowledge base

The company considers itself to be knowledge intensive, rather than information intensive; in other words, to operate effectively it relies heavily on individuals' knowledge and expertise rather than on information. The company does generate a great deal of information, but it is not managed very effectively, and this has led to some instances of duplication.

Knowledge transfer

Expert knowledge is communicated verbally within the organization, so employees need to be familiar with the structure of the company, and the functions of the departments within the company, in order to find where knowledge is held. An employee with a problem will often have to go looking for the right person to talk to. This can cause problems as well as being time consuming.

Information transfer

Information is transferred within the company in a number of ways. Some internal information about the company is circulated automatically to relevant departments; this does not include information about competitors or the marketplace in general. Most information is circulated on paper, but some parts of the business, especially the one dealing with dairy products, use the e-mail system.

Problems locating information

Problems locating information are frequent. A common problem is finding the right person with the right information, and ensuring that person understands the request.

Information ethos

The culture of the company emphasizes the importance of generating profit, so information relating to profit performance is valued highly. The value of other types of information, however, is not conveyed to workers effectively. The company recognizes this as a problem and is attempting to improve the situation. A new initiative is looking at ways of letting people know what information is already available to them, as well as encouraging them to go out and look for information.

Information and business objectives

The company's business objectives are to continue to improve the prospects of shareholders, employees and the communities in which they operate. It also aims to develop real partnerships with its customers, involving them fully in new product development. Within the group different companies have their own specific objectives. For example, one of the food company's objectives is innovation in recipe dish development, while the dairy company aims to be the lowest-cost producer and distributor in the industry. All the business objectives are designed to maximize profits and increase return to shareholders.

The company's information systems support these business objectives effectively. They enable the company to reduce its operating costs, while providing adequate market information. The systems are flexible enough to allow the company to respond to a hanging market.

Training and human resources

The company makes considerable effort to train staff in IT and information skills. However, most of this effort is concentrated on staff from the lower end of the business, and not enough is spent on more senior staff. Some of the company's executives cannot be described as information-literate, and the company recognizes this is one area that needs to be improved. The company has open learning resources and uses PC-based training for staff development.

In general, staff fall into two categories; those who are proactive will ensure they are aware of all the information resources available to them; others need to be told what is available. The company is investigating ways of ensuring that this second category is better informed.

Company E

Company profile

Company E is involved in the provision of a range of banking and other financial services. It has an annual turnover in excess of £3,000 million and employs over 67,000 staff.

Success factors

The company believes it is very successful when judged in relation to its stated objective of generating shareholder value. It has a return on capital in the median quartile range. When compared with other banks and the financial service industry in general, the bank is also very successful. It is seen as the most profitable of the big high street banks, and its CEO is respected in the industry.

Aside from financial measures, the bank has been an industry leader in introducing technology and in changing working practices. It was an early innovator in cashpoint and front office graphical user interfaces. The bank also feels it has a culture that has enabled change to be implemented effectively.

Reasons for success

The company believes the following factors have contributed to its success:

- a forward looking CEO driving the business
- effective use of IT to drive down operating costs
- efficient logistical planning
- a conservative, yet innovative approach to business

The CEO has pursued a policy of investing in business units which generate shareholder value independently. In this way resources have been allocated effectively to the various business segments. The CEO has also introduced an IT strategy which has lowered the cost of the company's operating base, making it more competitive. The company has successfully implemented effective information systems across its extensive branch network and believes it has managed the logistics of this better than its main competitors.

Although it has been innovative in its approach to business, the company has a cautious, conservative approach to diversification. Some business decisions have taken the financial sector by surprise. For example, when the industry was deregulated in 1986, the company did not commit itself too heavily in other financial services, and so was not forced to pull out, unlike many of its rivals.

Measures of success

The company uses a number of success measures. Quality of management is regarded as a very effective measure, along with financial soundness, innovation and strategic thinking. Export success is not applicable to the company, and environmental responsibility is not considered important.

Customer service and customer retention are rated highly. Financial measures are important, the main financial target being a Return on Capital Employed (ROCE) of greater than 18 per cent. The company makes use of quality standards, and has been quality assessed by the DTI; certain targets are set each year for the separate operating units.

Competitors

The company has a large number of competitors. The financial services industry was deregulated in 1986, opening up the industry and allowing previously separate sectors to compete with each other. The company would list its competitors as the other five retail banks, the building societies, and other niche competitors.

The other retail banks offer a similar range of products and services and are similar in size to company E. Although they are smaller, building societies also offer similar products and services and compete for the same customers. The marketplace appears to be saturated, with too many products chasing too few customers, so the company has been putting more emphasis on customer retention, in addition to attracting new customers.

Possibly the greatest threat will come from new entrants to the market, the so-called niche players, which concentrate on one area of the business and use technology to deliver a service with relatively low operating costs. One example is a credit card scheme launched by a large car manufacturer. The car manufacturer has collected a great deal of customer information through the business of selling cars and can target those customers who are likely to take up the credit card. This scheme is financed by another retail bank and may take customers away from company E. If such niche players are successful they may extend their product range and will then start to threaten other, larger financial service companies.

The company has information systems in place to monitor aspects of the market—its own performance, which it measures very effectively, the performance of its main competitors, and market conditions in general. This is done by means of a competitor analysis system and economic units which monitor the general state of the market. In general a lot of research is carried out into the economic environment and what the market wants. The company collects and analyzes a great deal of external data to enable it to monitor these variables.

The company also monitors levels of customer service, at present on an *ad hoc* basis, before the implementation of a formal customer monitoring service soon to be put in place. This will collect information on the point of service over the lifetime of the customer relationship; the information will be held centrally, and will be used to help improve levels of service and retain existing customers.

Since it is going through a process of restructuring, rationalizing its workforce, and re-engineering business processes, the company is monitoring the impact of these changes both on the organization and its customers—how employees will adapt to and accept the changes, and whether the customer will be satisfied with the level of service provided.

Information technology and information systems

The company believes three factors are critical to its survival, all of which depend on effective information technology and effective information systems: product innovation, speed of change, and customer satisfaction. The financial services industry relies on information technology in so many ways that it is now an essential part of the way the industry works. The essence of the industry is processing information; it produces very few tangible products. If a company is not an effective information processor it will be shut out of the market. The company is therefore very aware of the importance of effective information systems and the value of information.

User involvement

There are two classes of user in the company: those in head office, and those in the branches. In general the head office users are more involved in the systems design process. The company feels the balance should shift, with more emphasis on the branch users. Some users are taken out of the branch/business environment to become more closely involved in the systems design process. They are organized in Business Systems groups and take part in usability labs providing feedback to the Business Systems Design group.

One problem with involving users is that they are not always aware of what they want. The bank recognizes the danger of relying too heavily on what can be poorly conceived user requirements when designing information systems solutions.

Information technology

The company has carried out some experiments with expert systems with mixed results. They have been applied to the credit-scoring process (assessing the credit-worthiness of individuals and companies); although the results have been interesting, expert systems are not widely used in this role. They are used to support a help desk function and have been found to be fairly effective here.

A management information system has recently been put in place, with the emphasis on getting information across the whole retail banking function. The system is still developing and is not yet considered very effective. However, the company plans to include core operating statistics describing customer service, and this may make it more relevant to its users. One problem with this system, and with Executive Information Systems (EIS) in general, has been described as the 'comic book effect'; if the EIS is manufactured separately from the data then it will be less effective than if it were linked directly to the real data.

The company uses e-mail widely within the head office, but not in the branch network. Some users are more enthusiastic than others, perhaps because the culture of the organization has been one of face-to-face communication. This may be changing; the company has found that there is a growing demand for e-mail, although its use is not as widespread as in other organizations.

The company has been using voice mail for some time and has found it effective. A pilot study has started recently to investigate voice input for text but has not been very successful, perhaps because the technology for voice recognition is not yet effective. Videoconferencing is used widely and has proved effective for communicating between the company's head offices.

Information strategy

The company has high level strategies for all business areas. It relies so heavily on information technology that a number of information strategies are required: there are separate information system strategies for the branches, head office, treasury and every other bank function. The company has to deal with both inherited, legacy strategies and future strategies, and consequently with the trade-off between the two. One of the complexities of a large organization is having to manage such multiple strategies.

In theory, the information technology employed in providing information solutions is determined by the formal business planning process. In reality, account also has to be taken of what people actually want, so there is a degree of tension between the formal business plan and people's enthusiastic plans.

Essentially, though, investment in information technology is no different from any other investment and involves a very formal structured process, or applications development plan. A great deal of time is spent assessing all the financial and non-financial aspects of making an investment in IT. This process takes place at a senior level and decisions are made from a business perspective.

Evaluating information systems

Information systems have been introduced primarily to reduce the company's cost to income ratio, and this element is measured closely. The company points to a direct correlation between levels of investment in IT and decreasing head count in the branch network.

Other variables are harder to measure. The company has a benefit measuring group; when a new information system is introduced the group looks at the benefits and savings the system was designed to achieve and measures these against actual savings and benefits.

The company knowledge base

The company considers itself to be information intensive. However, individuals' knowledge is also considered to be important to the company's continued success. In the past it has relied heavily on individual knowledge of processes and customers. Now that the financial industry is more competitive this information needs to be held in a form that will enable more people to access it.

The company now processes a vast amount of information which is increasingly held on systems. Individuals are still required to search and analyze this information, and the company feels it only benefits when a new opening, service or product is identified. The key to utilizing information effectively lies in its analysis and management; information systems are therefore seen as a tool to support management and staff in the execution of the business.

Information resources

The company has a main library based in the economics department of its retail banking head office, a number of libraries in various locations across the bank, and an information centre in its second head office. The main library supports all the business functions within the company. The bulk of its work is maintaining its journal collection. The library did have a number of CD-ROM subscriptions, but these did not prove to be very useful and were cancelled. The main users of the library facilities come from the economics department. Other users include: treasury, trade and project finance, corporate banking, the Chief Executive's Office, private banking, and financial services.

The library has a database catalogue system known as PACE which contains details of the book and serial collection. It can be searched by classified number and classification description. At the moment this system is only available in the library, but there are plans to bring it online in the near future. The system was designed in conjunction with the library and the information systems department. A commercially available software package was adapted in-house to meet the individual requirements of the library and the existing software platform. The company makes use of one external online database, *FT Profile*.

The library provides a fortnightly library bulletin with details of newly catalogued books, pamphlets, reports, and indexed articles. It also circulates some periodical titles, mostly within the economics department. A small amount of internal information is circulated.

The library provides no formal training in information skills to the rest of the company. Any training that is given is on request. In general the library is a well established system that provides the company with valuable information.

Knowledge transfer

The expert knowledge of individuals is communicated both formally and informally. The company is very traditional and most communication is face-to-face and verbal. Recent reductions in the workforce have resulted in some knowledge being lost from the company. However, with the rapid development and implementation of information systems some of this knowledge is already out of date.

The company feels it can learn to do without certain types of knowledge, and some information can be codified and put into a readily accessible form. Knowledge is also communicated through training. Within the branch environment specific people have the responsibility for training staff in basic processes. More intensive training is provided at training centres.

Knowledge is communicated formally online, via the company's e-mail system, and there are presentations and a variety of meetings and conferences where knowledge can be communicated to groups of staff. The company also has centres of expertise; people with expert knowledge of particular processes are grouped together and given the responsibility for passing this knowledge on to other staff members.

Information transfer

The company has an established business circulation system, with information categorized for security risks. This takes the form of lists of topics and a database of notes from which people can select topics that are of interest to them. Information is also transferred within the head office on the company's e-mail system. This takes the form of lists of titles from which documents can be ordered. There is also a large amount of paper circulated within the company.

External information is also circulated. Market surveys carried out by competitors are collected and circulated to relevant departments. The company has a MIT system that sends synopses of articles to relevant staff members. Some technical literature is circulated, both whole journals and title pages. Individual departments also collect external information if they feel it is relevant to their work.

Problems locating information

Staff experience a number of problems locating information once it is inside the company. Some employees may not know the information they require is already available somewhere in the company. For example, a staff member approached an information systems specialist in the company with a request for a certain type of financial analysis tool, unaware that it was already available on his desktop PC. This sort of problem is common in the company. A great deal of information-gathering—knowing whom to approach and what to ask—depends on the individual's knowledge of the company which can only be acquired after a considerable amount of time.

Information held in electronic form and available online is, in contrast, relatively easy to find.

Information ethos

The company has tried to create a culture that emphasizes the importance of looking after its customers. To do this, staff members must have information about the customer, and in this way they learn the value of information. In the banking environment the value of information is also conveyed through the rules and regulations that govern the work of the bank.

Information and business objectives

The company's key business objectives can be summarized as:

- generate shareholder value
- increase market share
- ROCE greater than 18 per cent
- 'focus on things we do well, and do these better than anyone else'

The main objective is that of generating shareholder value. Within this there is an emphasis on fostering a sense of value among customers, maintaining good relationships with the community and staff development. Different departments within the company have additional objectives; the IT department, for example, aims to do things 'better, cheaper, faster' than their competitors.

In assessing how well information systems are designed to meet these objectives, the company focuses on five specific priority areas:

- quality of service
- ability to remodel branch environment
- operational support
- market gaining
- quality relation

All new applications are mapped against these objectives.

Training and human resources

The company feels it puts considerable effort into training all staff members in IT and information skills. However, the training is not designed to create overall experts, but rather to equip staff with only those skills necessary to do their job effectively.

Training materials, including laser-disk and PC-based materials, are available in branches for self-paced learning. Other materials are kept at the head offices and are available on demand. The head offices also have their own training centres, as do some larger branches. The company sponsors staff for the professional qualification of the Institute of Bankers, and for some approved MBA courses. The company also allows staff to work flexible hours, or to do homeworking, both of which have attracted people who want to follow educational courses.

In general, the company feels that staff are not aware of all the information resources that are available to them. However, there are moves to change the traditional, hierarchical structure of the company, and to use information to do this; there are moves towards providing information to empower the providers of service. This is a change the company acknowledges is necessary, but it will be a difficult one for an organization as large as company E to make.

Company F

Company profile

Company F is a large manufacturer of float glass products with annual profits of around £100 million and over 40,000 employees. It is based in the UK, and has operating units in over 20 countries supplying building, transport and other products.

Success factors

The company is seen to be very successful and can be described as a world leader in the manufacture of glass products. The glass and construction markets have been depressed in recent years and this has affected the company's performance. However, the UK market has shown signs of steady recovery in the last twelve months and the company is confident about its future success in the industry.

Reasons for success

Development of the float glass process and its subsequent exploitation have contributed to the company's success. It has also been successful in acquiring overseas operational units, especially in the southern hemisphere, in South America and Australasia.

The company continues to invest in the development and application of technology to provide new products and to improve the manufacturing efficiency of its operating units. It has ensured its continued success by the effective management of products and by reducing operational costs.

Measures of success

The company believes quality of management is necessary for success, in particular a management structure that is facultative and forward looking. Financial soundness, quality of products and services, and the capacity to innovate are also important.

The company does not rate export success highly; it concentrates its energy building up businesses abroad, rather than exporting tangible products. Environmental responsibility is not considered to be a contributor to the company's success, although it does invest heavily in ensuring its operating units conform to environmental legislation. Indeed, the company was recently awarded a top environmental award by the European Commission.

The company uses a number of other financial measures, of which growth and productivity are the most important.

Competitors

The company operates in a number of industry sectors, manufacturing and architectural being the most important. In the manufacturing industry they have seven or eight major and several smaller competitors. Other business interests have their own competitors. The company's main rival in the manufacture of glass is a French company of similar size.

The company believes its information systems enable it to measure aspects of the market effectively, including its own performance, the performance of its main competitors and the state of the market in general. It also monitors productivity and innovations in the industry, and since changes in legislation around the world can affect the company, it has information systems to monitor environmental and safety legislation.

Information technology and information systems

Information systems enable the company to reduce its costs, streamline the business and improve customer service. They also provide the company with the ability to manage effectively a range of business interests in 20 countries.

Information technology

The company makes effective use of expert systems to support business functions. An Executive Information System (EIS) provides information to the company decision makers but is regarded as neutral in its effect as an information service.

E-mail is used very effectively to communicate information within the company. The company makes effective use of automatic ordering and supply systems and dedicated networks. Electronic data interchange systems are well established within the company but their effect as information systems is seen as neutral.

Because company F's business interests are spread over a wide geographic area videoconferencing technology is widely used.

Decision on the technology to be developed for information systems are based on user requirements. Departments approach the group information systems department with a request for a new system to satisfy an identified business requirement. User requirements are then rationalized in line with the group policies and standards.

Information strategy

The company has what it describes as a 'partial' information strategy. It has identified common technological platforms for communications and desktop provision and is now investigating ways of looking across different business areas to enable cross-firm, or inter-company working, in line with business need.

Evaluating information systems

The company does not have a formal systems evaluation process. Rather, this is done on an *ad hoc* basis. Any assessment carried out examines how effectively the system meets the business objectives it was designed to support.

The company knowledge base

The company considers itself to be knowledge intensive, requiring individuals' knowledge and expertise to remain successful.

Information resources

The company has a central, corporate library which serves all the departments in the company, although the main users come from the business function—marketing, planning and sales. There are no other library sites in the company; some departments may have small collections of reference materials, but these are not organized.

The library subscribes to over 300 journals, 90 per cent of which cover technical subjects. The library makes limited use of CD-ROMs which, again, are mostly used to provide technical information to the company. The departments that make most regular use of the facilities come from group planning, on the business side, and research and development on the technical side of the company.

The library produces two current awareness bulletins (CAB), containing bibliographic details of indexed articles: one, covering business information, is produced weekly; a technical bulletin is produced fortnightly. The library offers an occasional selective dissemination of information (SDI) service. This is limited by lack of staff—the library has seen its workforce diminish in recent years. The library also offers a number of on-demand services, for example searches of online databases.

The library is networked to the rest of the company, but this is only used for e-mail communication at present. There are plans to use e-mail to distribute an electronic version of the current awareness bulletins, but they must first overcome the problem of an operating platform that is not compatible with the rest of the organization.

The library does not have its catalogue on a computer system, but plans to do so. Two database systems hold information on the current awareness bulletins, going back to 1986; one holds the business CAB, while another (incompatible) database holds the technical CAB details. The databases, which hold abstract information and are searchable, are held on two standalone PCs using different software packages. The library does plan to put the databases online to be accessible to the rest of the company, but has been unable to raise sufficient funds to do so.

The library subscribes to a number of online database providers. For technical information the library uses *Dialog, STN, Datastar* and *Orbit*, and for business information *Dun and Bradstreet online, Textline* and *FT Profile*. The library advertises its services on a company e-mail bulletin board and on the back of the CAB, and occasionally does presentations to departments within the company. The library circulates some information within the company, mostly business journal circulation, and also acts as a distribution point for internal research reports. The company estimates that around 25 per cent of staff are regular library users, another 50 per cent are aware of the library's existence, and the remaining 25 per cent are not aware the library exists. In general the library feels it could contribute more to the success of the company by extending its range of information services, but it needs more funding to be able to do this.

Knowledge transfer

The company encourages staff to produce internal reports and documentation about current developments and manufacturing processes. Knowledge is also communicated on a basis of need and there is provision for promulgation of best demonstrated practice in certain areas. Some knowledge is systematized, and the company makes some use of expert systems.

Information transfer

No information is circulated automatically to departments within the company. The e-mail system is used for internal communications and videoconferencing is used for communicating with other operating units.

Problems locating information

Staff do sometimes encounter problems locating information once it is inside the company. Information is stored in different ways, and may be held in different places, which makes finding the exact location of information very difficult. The company has no systems that enable information to be stored and retrieved effectively.

Information ethos

The company believes staff should only be made aware of information that is relevant to their work and makes no effort to ensure all staff are aware of the value of information. In general, information is conveyed on a 'need-to-know' basis. The company is very security conscious, and material considered confidential is only accessible to senior management. Information is filtered through the vertical, hierarchical structure and most information remains at a relatively high level.

Information and business objectives

The company's key business objective is to become and remain the leading producer and processor of glass in the building and automotive industries. To achieve this it has taken steps to reduce operating costs and generate cash flow. In addition, it has implemented a programme of selective investment to strengthen the core flat and safety glass business in order to reinforce the company's market position.

The company's information systems are designed to help achieve these objectives by providing an appropriate global infrastructure for the business. The company also aims to deliver appropriate systems to support business functions.

Training and human resources

The company makes some effort to provide all staff with appropriate training in IT and information skills. Training is seen as an integral part of delivering, maintaining and supporting systems. The company has a training centre based at its corporate head office site. Senior staff are provided with one-to-one training.

In general, staff are not aware of all the information resources that are available to them. The company believes this is not necessary for staff to do their work.

Company G

Company profile

Company G is a large high street retail fashion chain with 300 stores in the UK. It also runs a catalogue mail order service, is a retail distributor of household furnishings, and deals in financial services. The company's main operations are in the UK, with some overseas investment, notably in America. It has an annual turnover in excess of £300 million and employs over 9,000 staff.

Success factors

The company is very successful, with a strong brand image, a solid customer base, and a good reputation in the marketplace. After experiencing serious problems in the late 1980s, the management team has changed and the operation has been restructured. The company undertook these changes before the retail recession forced its competitors to do the same and this has put it in a good position to deflect some of the worst effects of the downturn.

Reasons for success

The company believes it is successful because it is good at the basics—putting the right product in the right place at the right time. This has involved a great deal of market research, understanding the market before launching the product range.

Measures of success

The primary measure of success used is financial soundness. All other measures are subservient to this or contribute to it. The company believes that using technology in an innovative way can contribute to success, but this means using tried and tested technology rather than being at the cutting edge.

The quality of products and services is important, but does not in itself lead to business success. Likewise, the ability to think strategically, export success and environmental responsibility are regarded as contributions to financial success, rather than as measures in themselves.

The company does have a number of different variables against which it monitors business performance. These are, in the main, additional financial measures. An example is the level of sales per square foot; if this increases then return on capital is also increased. The company is also making an effort to measure the level of customer service, but admits more effort is needed in this area.

Competitors

The company cannot name a direct competitor. Instead, a series of competitors, ranging from large high street chain stores to smaller niche companies, offer products that overlap with some of the retail areas served by company G.

The company's information systems enable it to monitor its own performance effectively, but not the performance of its main competitors or changes in the market generally. The company's systems collect information on a number of variables related to marginal costs of operations, but this information is not always processed and analyzed so that it can be used by decision makers. For example, the company does not monitor the profile of demand on sales within a particular store over a given period of time, although information relating to this is collected.

Information technology and information systems

The company regards its information systems as an important platform on which to build future business opportunities; the right foundation of systems helps create competitive edge. In other words, it needs flexible systems and effective systems development mechanisms in order to absorb changes in the business quickly. For example, the company has recently set up a new operation selling toiletries in cooperation with an American-based retail organization and was able to open the new stores within four months of signing the deal. This would not have been possible without a foundation of effective and flexible information systems.

User involvement

The company attempts to involve the user in every stage of the systems development process, from the initial concept, right through to purchasing the software package, redevelopment of the package to meet user requirements, and the final implementation of the system.
This has not always been the case. In the early 1980s the company went through a period of crisis; systems work was concentrated on 'fire-fighting', and as a result users were not consulted at all. The company is now coming out of this crisis and more effort is being made to take the steps described above. To facilitate this the company has set up a business development department, consisting of senior managers from operational functions whose role is to discuss with the business their IT requirements and to develop systems that will support the business.

Information technology

The company is investigating the use of neural networks to support operational functions and believes they will be very effective. It is also testing an Executive Information System (EIS) and e-mail; initial results indicate they will not be very effective at communicating information within the company.

Still at a very early development stage is the possibility of using an audio response unit to support directory operations, which will have the capacity to recognize customers' telephone orders. Videoconferencing is also under investigation and is likely to be very effective with respect to overseas operations.

The company has developed a 3-D design system for stores which provides designers with a full visualization of what a store will look like, saving time and resources. A work-flow system called Product Data Management has also been implemented. This enables fashion designers to design a garment complete with original sketches, diagrams and documentation, providing a complete pack of merchandizing information to the business.

The company has a formal procedure to identify which applications are to be developed for information systems. Essentially, information systems are developed to fulfil a recognized business need. The business requirements are first prioritized against business objectives and available resources. The next stage involves a business design process, and during this stage user requirements are defined. Here the options generally include buying a package, developing a package in-house, bringing in outside contractors to develop a system, or a mixture of the three. The system must meet the user's need, taking into account certain technical constraints, and must be compatible with the company's existing operating platform.

Information strategy

A company information strategy is currently under development. It will concentrate effort on developing information systems rather than operational systems. The operational systems have been in place for a number of years and are effective. The company now needs to develop systems to provide and analyze information effectively. The aim is to develop an open systems environment, based around UNIX, that is fully integrated with the company's existing mainframe systems.

Evaluating information systems

There is no formal systems evaluation process. At present technical staff rely on users to inform them if a particular system is not performing very well, or if the benefits delivered do not meet their expectations. The company is looking at implementing a formal system for post-evaluation of projects which examines the effectiveness of projects from both a business and a technical perspective. The company notes that business and IT are so reliant on each other that it is now difficult to examine one aspect without the other.

The company knowledge base

The company feels its success is due mainly to the knowledge and expertise held within the company, but there is no formal mechanism to make this information accessible. In order to improve this situation the company is developing an Executive Information System (EIS) built around the concept of information warehousing. This will attempt to pull together information sources that are held on different systems and make it accessible via the company network. At the moment the company's information systems hold a great deal of information that is not processed. The EIS will allow decision makers to access this information and manipulate it using fourth generation software tools.

Information resources

There is no formal company library or information centre. Individual departments may have their own collections of information resources. For example, the business development department has a small collection of reference materials, including a number of CD-ROMs and videos, and also purchases a number of management books and periodicals. Departmental staff scan periodicals for relevant articles, which they photocopy and pass to other members of staff. The personnel department has a similar collection of resources.

Knowledge transfer

There is no formal communication of expert knowledge within the company. Instead, people are expected to take hold of opportunities, get involved and seek advice from more senior staff members. People are expected to work as a team, and the company believes this encourages the informal communication of knowledge and expertise.

Knowledge is also communicated by on-the-job training and by monthly meetings where staff are encouraged to discuss their work with staff from different departments.

Information transfer

Internal information, mainly report-based sales information, is communicated online, or more commonly as a paper print out, and is passed to departments on a daily basis. The company e-mail system is not used effectively for internal communications.

External information is circulated on an *ad hoc* basis. A large part of this information is collected informally by staff working on their own initiative.

Problems locating information

Problems commonly occur when contacting a department that is located away from the main headquarters. More serious problems arise when attempting to extract information from the company's mainframe. There are software tools available which are designed to extract information from the mainframe and put it into a form that can be used on a PC, but these are rudimentary and often corrupt the data.

Information ethos

Because of the recent troubled history of the company, staff members have concentrated on the operational side of the business, rather than spending time developing systems that would allow information to be used more effectively and in more innovative ways. However, this attitude is changing slowly, helped by the CEO who is promoting the value of information within the company.

Information and business objectives

The company's primary business objective is to make money for its shareholders; all other objectives contribute to this. The company's information systems are therefore designed to lower operating costs in order to maximize profits.

To be successful the company must get the right products to the right customer at the right price and its information systems are designed to enable it to do this effectively and cheaply. On the operational side of the business this means getting stock to the stores in a timely manner. On the management side it means providing decision makers with information about sales and trends that will enable them to plan future seasons effectively. The systems that support customer service enable the company to collect information on its customers so it can provide products that match their tastes and requirements. Computer aided design systems support the designers and enable them to work more effectively. All the company's systems are integrated in terms of the business, rather than necessarily in terms of the technology.

Training and human resources

In the past training has been neglected, but now the company is putting a lot of effort into this area. All staff in head office are provided with training in IT skills to enable them to use the applications on their PCs. Training tends to focus on operational requirements; workers in the retail outlets are provided with training in the use of the cash tills that are actually PC based, with a PC back office.

The company organizes a number of training courses, both internal and external, to train staff in general applications or more specialist software systems. Staff are also encouraged to take part in external training courses to learn new skills, or to upgrade old ones. The company also organizes personal development courses and management courses.

In general staff members are not aware of all the information resources that are available to them. One reason for this is a lack of training in general information-seeking skills. The business is just beginning to recognize the potential value of encouraging staff to look for information.

Company H

Company profile

Company H is a medium sized life insurance company, based in Scotland, operating throughout the UK and with an operating unit on the Isle of Man.

Success factors

The company rates itself as above average in the insurance industry but, because it is one of the smaller companies in the market, it is difficult to say that it is very successful. However, when measured against other companies of a similar size, company H is very successful.

Reasons for success

The company believes a number of factors have contributed to its success. Perhaps foremost among these is the fact that the company is a subsidiary of a larger building society group which gives it access to existing retail outlets and an existing customer base on which to build. Another important factor is the quality of the people who work in company H. Taken together, these two factors have enabled Company H to expand its customer base from around three million to over three billion customers in a period of four to five years. Part of this growth is due to acquisition of other businesses, rather than true organic growth. Being part of a larger group has given the company a solid financial base that has allowed it to make such acquisitions.

Measures of success

The company rates quality of management, the capacity to innovate, and strategic thinking as useful measures of success. Quality of products and services and financial soundness are also considered very useful.

In the main the company measures its success in financial terms, primarily in terms of turnover and return to shareholders. Beyond this, measures tend to be geared towards levels of customer service and industry awards.

Competitors

The company has a large number of competitors which fall into four distinct groups:

- insurance companies
- life and pension companies
- fund management companies
- banks and building societies

Within this, further distinctions can be made, for example 'like for like' competitors, i.e. insurance companies of a similar size to company H, and larger insurance companies. Another category is niche players—companies that compete with company H in one product area, for example fund management. Another way of classifying the competition is to look at those that compete with regulated and non-regulated products.

The Financial Services Act of 1986 had the effect of tightening the framework that governs regulated products while at the same time relaxing the rules governing which companies should be allowed to trade in such products. This had the dual effect of opening up the marketplace to new entrants while increasing the cost of trading in regulated products.

The company has established information systems that enable it to monitor various aspects of its own performance, the performance of its competitors, and general changes in market conditions.

Information technology and information systems

The company believes that the way information technology is used to provide information systems and services can have a profound effect on its performance.

Because the company has grown through acquisition it has inherited a number of systems that are expensive to maintain and even more expensive to replace. They are outdated, take up a lot of processing time, operate on different platforms and are incompatible with the rest of the company's information systems. The company believes that this puts it at a disadvantage.

A further problem is that the older systems were designed to provide information about, and focus on, the product. The company's interests have shifted away from this to focus on customer requirements and customer satisfaction, but since an individual customer may invest in several products, information about that customer may be dispersed over a number of incompatible systems. The company is trying to improve this situation, but it is an ongoing process.

User involvement

The company tries to ensure users are involved in every stage of the logical and physical design of information systems. Every new system is assigned a project manager and a project sponsor, both of whom will come from a business function. This is important because the business project sponsor will ultimately hold the benefits, and should therefore be responsible for managing the delivery of those benefits. An information systems (IS) manager is responsible for the technical components of the system. The business and IS managers work together, not as customer and service provider, but as real partners. The project team involves both technical and business members, assisted by a business analyst, who together agree on the business requirements of the company. Before a system is developed a business requirement document is drawn up by the project team and submitted to the company. Only when this is agreed will the development process begin. Training is provided to staff who will use the system and they are consulted at every stage in the development process.

Information technology

The company uses e-mail for communication both within its head office and to communicate with its parent company and the retail branch network. This is judged to be effective, although the system currently in use is very old with limited distribution capabilities.

The company uses Electronic Data Interchange (EDI) systems to a limited extent. Where used they are effective. A pilot Executive Information System (EIS) has started which will provide sales information in a graphical form to the company's senior decision makers. Sales information is seen to be the lifeblood of the company, and the ability to notice trends in the market is vital to its success.

The EIS is being developed in recognition of the need to improve the way sales and market information is communicated to executives. In the past the company has produced paper based board reports, reproducing sales information as basic figures; when the same information is presented graphically it is far easier to understand and trends are identified easily. At the moment the EIS is built around a PowerPoint slide show. Before additional software tools are made available to enable executives to manipulate the data, a cost/benefit analysis will be conducted based on the pilot system.

The company also plans to develop a videoconferencing capability. The head office of the parent company is based in central England and travelling between the two head offices is very time consuming. The company feels videoconferencing will be an effective solution to this problem.

The company does not use expert systems or voice recognition systems. There are plans to develop a rule-based expert system for automatic underwriting.

The company has a formal planning procedure to identify the IT applications to be developed for the provision of information systems. This is done through the company planning process. Essentially, corporate planning objectives for the group are developed with one and five year corporate business objectives. These objectives are cascaded to individual companies within the group, including company H, and individual company priorities are identified.

Individual projects are identified from this process. The next stage should entail an individual cost/benefit analysis for each of the projects but the company admits it does not always carry this out. In practice, the company's corporate planning group, which consists of senior managers and the managing director, assigns priorities to each project, making sure it is line with one or more of the corporate business objectives. The projects are then prioritized relative to each other and a project list is developed, which forms the basis of the IS programme for the next twelve months.

Information strategy

The company does have an information systems strategy (ISS) which is under review. The company's ISS is a part of the parent building society's ISS; a new group ISS will be agreed in partnership with the parent company. The group ISS is seen as a true strategy, an outline of the principles and direction for the company to move towards in terms of information systems development.

A key element of the current ISS is to reduce the number of outmoded systems the company has inherited through acquisitions. The priority of the new group ISS will be to move the focus of information systems away from the product to the customer.

Evaluating information systems

The company does evaluate its information systems but recognizes that this is not done to the extent that it should be. There are post implementation reviews, but these tend to focus more on the delivery process rather than ensuring the business benefits claimed are actually achieved.

The company is starting to take steps to ensure the evaluation process examines all aspects of the effectiveness of the systems. A review proposal published recently has outlined a new procedure which takes into account a number of factors, including cooperation with internal audit to assess the business benefits claimed for information systems against the benefits delivered. The argument for taking this approach is that it will improve the processes supported by information systems, and thereby improve customer service and satisfaction.

The company knowledge base

The company considers itself both information intensive and knowledge intensive; it is necessary to have elements of both to be successful.

The company has no central, corporate library or company information centre. However, individual departments do have their own limited collections. These tend to be paper based, consisting of periodicals, books, and manuals, with some videos on specific topics.

Knowledge transfer

Individuals' knowledge and expertise are communicated to other members of staff both formally and informally.

People who are working together often acquire the same knowledge and skills, and these are passed from the senior member to the junior, from the experienced to the less experienced. There is a degree of informal on-the-job training. Managers and other staff members will also go looking for knowledge on topics they are unfamiliar with. For example, managers from operational functions will approach staff in technical areas for information on new developments in technology that may be applicable to their work. Formal communication of knowledge takes place through the company's extensive formal training schemes. Knowledge can also be communicated formally at staff meetings and regular staff briefings.

Information transfer

Internal information is transferred within the company at a number of levels. Within technology there is a monthly IS briefing session that ensures staff are aware of information about the business, divisional information, sales information, and other information that may be of interest. The e-mail system is used extensively for internal communication, both formal company information and informal social communications. E-mail will be used more widely when a new improved system is introduced.

External information is also circulated within the company, mostly on an informal basis. Staff circulate periodicals, technology reports, trade papers, and articles of interest on an *ad hoc* basis.

The company's marketing department does have a formal information gathering procedure. A member of staff is employed to scan periodicals and newspapers for articles that may be applicable to the company or the group. These are photocopied and put together in a pamphlet of 20-30 pages which is circulated to departments on a fortnightly basis.

Problems locating information

Within the company there are two types of users of information—active and passive. The first actively seek the information they require and know where to go for it, whereas passive users tend to wait until information is passed along the line. Active users are more likely to know when information is missing, but passive users do not know what information they are expected to have so may never be aware of any lack.

Information seekers at a senior level experience relatively few problems locating information. At a less senior level more problems tend to arise. The most common is knowing which department is likely to hold the information required; this demands experience of the company and personal knowledge of individuals' roles within it.

Information ethos

The company does not convey the value of information to its workers. Indeed, the true value of information is not fully understood by senior staff within the company. It is only when it is missing that information becomes an issue.

Information and business objectives

The company's business objectives can be summarized as:

- achieving the corporate mission statement
- improving customer service and customer satisfaction
- improving the financial health of policy holders and shareholders

There are separate objectives within individual functions of the company. For example, the information systems department's objectives are to reduce the costs of operations and processes.

The company's information systems must be geared to achieving one or more of the business objectives before they reach the development phase. The company is now looking to use information technology and information systems in more innovative ways, for example to drive up sales and profits, rather than simply reducing the cost of operations.

Training and human resources

The company measures the effectiveness of its training schemes by the number of training awards it has won. The company training department has developed a course directory on a wide range of subjects, funded by a central training budget. It runs the British Computer Society's personal development scheme, in addition to training support for current projects within the company. The IS department has its own training budget and provides additional training in IT and information skills to departments within the company. The training department, in association with the IS department, is developing an open learning multimedia training suite within the company head office.

The company also has a close association with a local university, and provides sponsorship to staff who will benefit from an external degree programme. Staff are currently sponsored on Masters courses, Diplomas and Bachelor degrees. The company is contributing to the funding of a financial services department within the university.

In general staff are well aware of all the information and training resources that are available to them.

Company I

Company profile

Company I specializes in the marketing, design, production and maintenance of custom-built software and hardware systems, consulting and project management, and the production of software products. The company employs over 3,400 staff, and has an average annual turnover in excess of £300 million. Approximately 52 per cent of profits come from business within the UK, with 30 per cent from the rest of Europe, 9 per cent from the US, and 9 per cent from the rest of the world.

Success factors

The company was founded over 20 years ago and in the early years was very successful. Indeed, in 1980 it was voted company of the decade. However, at the start of the 1990s it went through a period of decline, recording a post-tax loss in 1991. These problems were due in part to the world recession. The company has now reorganized its senior management structure and is aiming to repeat the success of the 1970s and 1980s. It describes the past four or five years as fairly average in terms of success, but now feels it has come through this period.

Reasons for success

The founders of the company ran it for the first 15 years. During this period the computer industry was booming, and the company was very successful. When the original management team left they were replaced by professional managers who lacked the entrepreneurial spirit of the originators. During this time the industry, and the company, went into decline due to a general recession. In the last twelve months a new management team has been brought in and the company believes it will repeat its early success.

Measures of success

The company rates quality of management and financial soundness as very useful measures of success. The capacity to innovate is also very useful, and is considered essential if the company is to compete in the technological market. Quality of products and services is less useful as a success measure, while strategic thinking is seen as neutral.

The company has a number of overseas operations and rates export success highly. However, it must be noted that the company does not define export success as the ability to sell products outside the UK. Instead, it concentrates its efforts on establishing operating units in other countries, and is therefore a truly international organization. The company considers environmental responsibility to be of little importance as a measure of success.

The company uses other financial measures when assessing its performance, including the absolute amount of sales achieved in a particular territory, or for a specified product. It also sets specific targets for its sales staff, and this is particularly important when developing an overseas operating unit. One non-financial measure is applied to managers; they are judged on their ability to retain staff—and thereby knowledge—rather than constantly having to replace these.

Competitors

The company faces a great deal of competition. The nature of its business means it competes in a number of different market sectors, niche markets and different geographical areas. The competition in each market sector is fierce, and this makes it very difficult to monitor. In general, competitors can be divided into four groups: first, second and third class competitors, and niche players.

First class competitors have a history similar to company I's: they were formed at about the same time, and operate in similar product and service areas. Second class competitors are from accountancy backgrounds which have moved into the information system consultancy market. Third class competitors are computer manufacturing companies that have entered the computer services market. Niche competitors specialize in one area of company I's business; they are numerous and very difficult to identify.

The company collects and analyzes market information, and has information systems that enable it to monitor both its own performance and the performance of other companies in the marketplace. It has invested a great deal of time and money in developing financial reporting systems and is able to monitor its own performance very effectively. The company is not at all effective, however, at monitoring its competitors, and not very effective at monitoring changes in the market generally. There are many market indicators available which enable the company to compare its own performance with that of the industry as a whole. However, it is unable to collect adequate information on its competitors.

Information technology and information systems

Company I recognizes that the effective use of information technology in the provision of information systems can greatly improve business performance. It believes that information systems can be used to increase a company's competitiveness within an industry if it is responsive to changes in that industry. The company's information systems have improved communication of information within the company, and as a result the pace of business has increased.

User involvement

The company puts a great deal of effort into involving users in the information system development process. It has a set of corporate applications that support finance, personnel, sales and marketing. When systems are designed to support one of these areas, the information systems (IS) department encourages the users to produce a system requirement document as a first step towards selecting the system. The company develops very few of its systems in-house, preferring to adapt existing software packages, so the next step involves the software package developer demonstrating various packages to the end users, so that they can select the one that matches their requirements. The package selected is then modified by the IS department, based on these requirements. The IS department also asks a representative group from the user department to test the new system and to contribute to the development process.

Information technology

The company makes extensive and effective use of electronic mail for internal communications. It does not have an Executive Information

System (EIS), although it has started a pilot scheme using technology developed for the World Wide Web to provide a hypertext database of company information to executives and other staff members. A pilot scheme has also commenced to test the effectiveness of videoconferencing technology, which it is hoped will facilitate communication with overseas operating units.

The process by which IT is selected for the provision of information systems is driven by the end user—senior functional managers or enthusiastic line managers. There is a formal process for allocating funds to systems development. However, the selection process is rather less formal and depends largely on the enthusiasm of the project sponsor. In other words, the company takes a bottom-up approach to systems development, with an element of 'whoever shouts loudest get what they want'. The company recognizes that a top-down approach would be more effective.

Information strategy

The company does not have an information strategy, but is working towards developing one. It does have a standard framework of technology which future applications must adhere to; this is one element of the future strategy. This framework describes the physical infrastructure of the company's technological base. For example, the company has no mainframe systems, but operates in a client-server environment, with a UNIX base and Intel PCs running Windows as the client front-end; all future applications must therefore run under UNIX with a Windows front-end. Another aspect to the infrastructure is the decision to use existing software packages, rather than developing software in-house.

Evaluating information systems

The company recognizes the need for a systems evaluation process but does not yet have one. It is aware that older systems are failing and, when it becomes apparent that a system no longer functions effectively, it is replaced. The company is also aware when a system is performing very well, but there are no formal procedures to measure this.

The company knowledge base

The company believes it is knowledge intensive—it requires individuals' knowledge and expertise to remain competitive. The business is changing constantly, so staff need information about new developments to update their knowledge.

Information resources

The company has a small conventional library where a small number of books, periodicals and other reference materials are stored. It provides the company with a great deal of market research information, a large percentage of which is collected by searching online databases. The library also receives a large amount of external data both in paper form and electronically. The library is thus an important resource for the company.

Internally, the company holds a great deal of information. One problem has been that this information is stored in a variety of formats on different machines, with no effective way of retrieving it. To solve this problem the company has started a trial programme aimed at providing all staff with access to this rich mine of information. The experiment involves using software developed for the World Wide Web to format the information and allow staff access to it. A MOSAIC browser is used to view documents that have been formatted using the Hypertext Mark-up Language (HTML) over an internal network. Documents can be searched, and related documents can be recalled and displayed. This system is called 'Repository', and the experiment is proving to be very successful. Access restrictions can be applied to sensitive information. The system will be available on all networked PCs within the company.

Knowledge transfer

The company is aware of the danger of not transferring knowledge within the organization. During its financial difficulties a number of staff left, taking their knowledge and expertise with them. The company now attempts to transfer knowledge between individuals within the organization via training and documentation.

The company is engaged in a fundamental review which will examine, and if possible re-engineer, each business process, and produce documentation to describe it. The last review was over ten years ago, and the company feels it is time to update both the processes and the documentation.

Information transfer

A small amount of information is circulated to all staff on a regular basis, including a bi-monthly magazine which contains some internal information, with references to articles from relevant periodicals and magazines. The internal mail system is automated; staff can subscribe to mail lists and receive regular announcements. The company is looking at ways of encouraging more staff to use this service.

There is a newsnet-type interface for internal company discussion groups, which is organized for technical discussion between staff. At present this service is only available to staff in the UK and parts of the US, but there are plans to extend it to cover offices in the rest of the world.

The company also has an integrated telephone system for internal communication. All company offices in the UK, regardless of their location, are on the same London telephone exchange so that staff can communicate either verbally or via e-mail across the company network at zero cost. The company's e-mail system is used widely for internal communication and for transferring data files. Fax machines are also used to communicate between company offices and with external organizations.

Problems locating information

The company experiences a lot of difficulties locating information and this is the main reason why the 'Repository' system has been developed. One major problem is that company offices are spread over a wide geographic area, so information may be held in one part of the country that is needed in another. Another, more serious, problem is that a large number of staff work in client companies for long periods of time. Extending the company network into client companies would be difficult, and in many cases impossible.

Information ethos

The company does not convey the value of information to all workers effectively. This is a recognized problem and the company has embarked on a number of initiatives designed to improve this situation. One problem is the range of staff employed, from Ph.D computer scientists, who cannot understand why everyone does not have a workstation, to staff who have never used a computer.

Information and business objectives

The new CEO has defined new business objectives for company I. The main objective is to grow significantly faster than the market. The company aims to double in size in the next four years. Most of this growth is expected to occur in overseas markets where the company's presence is relatively small. The company is also aiming for absolute turnover growth, achieving this through more emphasis on sales and marketing, and increasing operating efficiency.

In terms of helping it meet these objectives, the company's current information systems are inadequate. In order to achieve this sort of growth the company will have to re-engineer its information systems. The current systems review and the future information strategy are part of this process.

Training and human resources

The company makes some effort to train staff in information and IT skills. Most members of staff receive at-the-desk instruction, or on-the-job training of some sort. The company does not organize a great deal of formal training for staff. Most training is organized by individual departments or individual operating units and is not controlled centrally. The company encourages this bottom-up approach.

In general the company recognizes that most staff members are not aware of all the information resources available to them and has started a series of seminars aimed at increasing awareness. One major problem is that staff are often away from the company for long periods of time working on contracts with client companies, or working in overseas operating units. Communicating changes in the company to these employees is very difficult.

The company also experiences problems communicating information because its head office is located in a number of buildings and staff are not aware of the electronic resources that can help them. When staff are fully informed about these resources the situation will improve.

Company J

Company profile

Company J is a large UK-based brewing and leisure company, with some interests in Holland and Belgium. It has an annual turnover in excess of £800 million.

Success factors

The company believes that in relation to the industry as a whole it is successful, bordering on very successful, with a return on capital in the upper-median quartile range. Its three main businesses are brewing, licensed retailing and short break leisure, which each contribute an equal share of the company's turnover.

Reasons for success

In the main the company has grown through acquisition, rather than organically. It once concentrated on brewing and selling off-the-shelf products, but in recent years has increased the number of its tied pubs and acquired a number of leisure businesses. The move into the leisure industry has been very successful and well timed, as the brewing industry is going through a period of change. The leisure business now contributes 32 per cent of the company's operating profit, the same as brewing.

The company's success is also attributed to successful management, the strong image of its products, and its commitment to training which improves the quality of service offered in the retail outlets.

Measures of success

The company regards financial soundness, quality of products and services, and the capacity to innovate as very useful measures of success. The quality of management and strategic thinking are also considered useful. Different measures are used for different businesses. On the whole these tend to be financial measures. For example, the retail business measures premium brand volumes as a percentage of total sales, while the leisure business measures the occupancy rates in its leisure outlets. The company also the measures the quality of its products and services across the range of its businesses.

Competitors

All the businesses operate in a very competitive market. The British brewing industry is arguably the most competitive in the world and many traditional brewing competitors have also moved into the leisure industry. The company has three main competitors among the large brewing companies, along with small local brewers that have been increasing in number in the last few years. In terms of the leisure industry, and more specifically the short break market, there are a large number of competitors.

The company's information systems enable it to monitor very effectively both its own performance and changes in market conditions generally. However, they are less effective at monitoring the performance of competitors.

Information technology and information systems

The company estimates that about 90 per cent of all business strategy is now based on its information systems and on information technology in general.

User involvement

A central computer department controls the development of information technology in the company, working with IT departments and user departments to provide IT support to the business.

The systems development process includes an element of user participation, the extent depending on the type of system involved. For example, a recent telesales system has been developed with the end users participating in every stage of the process. Users described what they wanted from the system and this formed the basis of a systems specification document written by the central computer department. Users commented on the specification and the central computer department wrote the software for the new system. The system was then tested on a trial basis by the user department, supervised by the local business systems department. This gave the users an opportunity to comment on the system and recommend any changes that could be made. However, this level of participation is not applied to all information systems; sometimes it is too expensive and sometimes managers requesting the system are unwilling to go through the process.

Information technology

Expert systems have been used at the company's head office and were judged to be very effective. The company has an effective Executive Information System (EIS) and makes extensive use of e-mail. At present the e-mail system is mainframe based, and so is only used to communicate within individual sites. However, the company plans to introduce an online system that would enable it to communicate between its different sites. The company does use automatic ordering and supply systems, and Electronic Data Interchange (EDI), but the impact these have on the business is considered neutral.

The IT selection and development process for smaller systems is rather informal. The manager concerned contacts the local business systems department with a request outlining what is needed. These requests are collected locally and prioritized in line with business needs. The business systems department will then provide IT solutions for smaller projects, while decisions about larger projects are made centrally. One problem with this informal approach has been a duplication of effort. Larger information systems decisions, for example the development of warehousing systems, are made centrally by senior executives. Projects are prioritized on the basis of business need.

Information strategy

The company does not have an identifiable information strategy at the present time.

Evaluating information systems

The company does have an evaluation process. Information systems are generally introduced to replace an existing procedure; a new system's performance is measured against the data relating to the original procedure.

This evaluation process is conducted automatically on all new systems. There is no set procedure, but individual departments undertake evaluation as a matter of course.

The company knowledge base

The company believes its success depends on both information and individuals' knowledge and expertise, but emphasizes the importance of individuals' ability to sell products. The company regards information relating to sales and performance as largely historic. It is the day to day operations of the company that ensure its success.

The company has a central library facility where information is stored.

Knowledge transfer

Individuals' knowledge and expertise are not communicated effectively to other members of staff. Often the company does not appreciate the value or the importance of individuals' knowledge until they leave.

Information transfer

Information relating to sales and company performance and individual businesses within the company is circulated daily, mostly on paper. Some information is directed at certain individuals, but most is circulated to all staff. Some information is also circulated on the e-mail system, but this only operates within individual company sites, so cross-site communication is limited to telephone and fax.

External information is circulated at the discretion of the individual managers concerned. This tends to be based on what managers consider the people in their department need to know to do their work.

Problems locating information

Staff experience some serious problems locating information once it is inside the company. The main problem is that staff do not know which individuals or departments are likely to hold certain types of information. For example, three departments are responsible for setting up new business accounts; these are based at three different geographic locations, so getting information about new accounts can be very difficult. This sort of problem is common within the company.

Information ethos

The company has taken steps to create an environment that encourages staff to play a full role in its operations; there is a general feeling that it is everybody's company. One way this is done is through regular monthly briefings to all staff about company performance and market share.

Information and business objectives

The company's primary business objective is to make money—to increase market share and so increase profits. By providing sales information that can be used to identify trends in the market the company's information systems help it to meet this objective. For example, systems on the brewing side of the business collect data on consumption trends and types of sales outlets.

Training and human resources

The company makes some effort to train all staff members in IT and information skills, but the quality of training tends to vary from one part of the business to another. This is attributable to different priorities—some parts of the company place more value on training and staff development than others.

The company has a number of training centres at different locations providing training in IT and management topics. It also has online tutorials for its software packages. Some money is available to sponsor staff on external courses, and some training is provided by outside agencies.

In general, the company realizes that all staff are not aware of the information resources available to them and this is largely due to a lack of resources.

Company K

Company profile

Company K is involved in the operation of tyre, exhaust and automotive retail and repair depots. It has 626 retail outlets throughout the UK, and in Holland, Belgium and Ireland. With an annual turnover of over £200 million, the company employs in excess of 3,000 people.

Success factors

The company is very successful and has seen sales grow by 34 per cent in the last five years. Compared with the industry, it has a return on capital in the upper-median quartile range, and return on total assets in the upper quartile range. Annual turnover has increased steadily in the last five years and the company has continued to expand its operations in the UK and the Benelux countries.

Reasons for success

The company identifies three factors that have contributed to its success: quality of service, quality of staff and customer satisfaction. These areas form the company's philosophy, as stated by the CEO over twenty years ago; the aim is to achieve customer satisfaction through quality of service and staff. Quality of customer service leads to customer loyalty and so ensures success. The company has recently been awarded two quality of service awards by readers of popular motoring magazines. It recognizes that staff are its most valuable asset; they are the only contact with the customers and so are key to the company's success.

This success in these areas is achieved through training and motivating staff in the retail centres. The company also requires effective management of a large number of operational units spread over a wide geographic area and this is achieved by the effective use of information systems that provide operational information to a fairly small administrative centre.

Measures of success

The company considers quality of management, financial soundness, quality of products and services, the capacity to innovate, and strategic thinking to be very useful measures of success. Export success is a useful measure, but environmental responsibility is regarded as neutral.

The main measures of success are levels of sales and profits, supported by measures of customer satisfaction. Customer satisfaction is monitored closely: every customer is provided with a Customer Satisfaction Card to complete and return; these cards are analyzed and the results are fed into a customer service system that ensures follow-up. This feedback is also included in a weekly in-house magazine, together with customers' letters and other comments.

The real measure of the company's success is reflected in its share price and its net worth, both of which have more than doubled in four years, indicating confidence in the company's continued success.

Competitors

The company has many competitors, ranging in size from large national retail outlets to small private garages. The number of companies similar in size to company K are limited to two or three in the UK.

The company's information systems enable it to monitor its own performance very effectively, but because it sees itself as a market leader, it is not interested in measuring the performance of its competitors, preferring to concentrate on maintaining the loyalty of existing customers.

Information technology and information systems

Information systems play a major role in the company's success. They increase the flow of information through the business, enabling effective management action. They also cut operational costs, which allows the company to offer low prices to its customers.

User involvement

The company's key information systems were developed in the early 1980s when users were deeply involved in their specification and development. The systems are focused on the needs of the business and support it well. Therefore, apart from some minor readjustments, the company has not sought to change its information systems a great deal in this time.

One major change has been the development of an electronic point of sales system (EPOS) for the retail centres. The EPOS system comprises management action terminals (MATs), based in the retail centres, and management action systems, based at headquarters. The MATs are seen as the keystone of the business. This system was developed with a great deal of input from end users and has proved to be very successful.

Information technology

The company uses an e-mail system to communicate between the head office and suppliers; this is considered effective. Its automatic ordering and supply systems are essential to the business and are rated very effective. The company also makes effective use of Electronic Data Interchange (EDI) systems.

The management action terminals are point of sale microcomputers, designed specifically for the company's operation. During the day the MAT supports the following operations:

- providing customer quotations
- producing cash sale invoices
- recording stock movements
- capturing time and attendance details
- authorizing credit card payments
- controlling banking
- providing managers with stock and sales information

Business information from the MATs is fed directly into the company's highly automated administration system. Each MAT is polled automatically by central information systems and details of the day's business are collected. This information updates the company's stock and sales database. New orders are generated automatically and transmitted by EDI to suppliers, enabling them to operate a 'just in time' delivery service. Supplier invoices are received electronically, and matched with delivery details on the MAT; payment details are transmitted via EDI to suppliers. Staff payments, credit card purchase information, and sales invoices are generated and transmitted automatically. In this way the company operates a highly automated, virtually paperless, management control system.

Information strategy

The company has no long term information strategy. It sees itself as a young, entrepreneurial company, constantly on the lookout for new opportunities; information systems allow it to exploit these opportunities. The company's information systems have the flexibility to support its growth through acquisition.

Evaluating information systems

The company does not evaluate its information systems formally. However, it regards the business benefits of the systems as obvious. For example, of more than 3,000 employees fewer than 500 work in administrative functions. The company's automated management systems eliminate the need for manual administration, allowing it to maintain a very low cost operation.

The company knowledge base

The company requires both information and expertise to remain competitive. It is competing in a market where products are similar, so to remain competitive it must collect market information to enable it to adjust its prices. Customer service is just as important as price; the company has a number of systems designed to measure levels of customer service and customer satisfaction. The company also feels the quality of staff training helps it remain competitive. Knowledge is passed on to less experienced staff through training.

The company has a centralized information centre, known as the quality management section, where control manuals are stored. This was introduced as part of its British Standard accreditation. Because its business is very simple, the company feels it does not require a large library or information centre.

Knowledge transfer

Knowledge is transferred in the company through staff training. Some formal training is carried out at the company training centre, but it is more usual for staff to receive on-the-job training. The company has an apprenticeship scheme that lasts two years and leads to a City and Guilds qualification in Automotive Parts and Fitting Skills. The company's training schemes have received an Investors in People Award.

Information transfer

The company believes in employee participation, and employees are kept fully informed on company activities. Internal information is circulated to all employees automatically. The company produces a daily newspaper and a weekly magazine, containing financial and other company information. There are regular staff briefing sessions, and all employees receive a copy of the company annual report. Almost half the workforce hold shares in the company through a share participation scheme.

Internal information is also communicated electronically via the e-mail and MAT systems. Each retail outlet has a 'master manager' who is responsible for running the centre. Information is conveyed to the master manager automatically via the MAT in the centre. In turn, the master manager can communicate information to headquarters in the same way. The company circulates very little external information.

Problems locating information

One major problem has been that information held in the company's database has been difficult to extract; it was designed to focus on operations, reducing administration, not to provide management information. This is a recognized weakness, and the company has been upgrading the system to correct it. The first stage involved the introduction of an ORACLE database with flexible user query tools. This will draw information from the operational database to provide management information.

Information ethos

The company encourages staff to view information and information technology as tools which they need to do their work.

Information and business objectives

The company's key business objective is to provide a service that will delight the customer. Other objectives are either designed to achieve this, or are results of achieving this. For example, the company is committed to staff training and staff development because staff are the initial contact with the customer.

Information systems are designed to enable staff to get on with the business without being concerned with administration. Before the MAT system was introduced, a centre manager would spend up to two hours a day doing book work; now the manager simply presses the 'end of day' button on the MAT and the administration work is done automatically.

Training and human resources

The company is committed to providing all staff with a high level of training, but makes little effort to train staff in information and IT skills. This is a deliberate policy: the company's information systems are designed to be simple to use, so staff do not require specific IT or information skills training.

In the head office staff receive a small amount of training in the use of simple software packages, word processors or spreadsheets. Staff do receive training in the skills they require to do their work. All centre staff take part in a two year apprenticeship training scheme leading to a recognized City and Guilds qualification, and staff are encouraged to update their skills regularly.

The company is a Founder Member of the Charter for Business and encourages staff to take part in the Duke of Edinburgh's Award Scheme to strengthen links with the community. It allows some staff to take external qualifications, for example MBA or other Masters degree.

In general, the company believes staff are aware of the information resources that are necessary to enable them to do their work.

Company L

Company profile

Company L is a group engaged in the origination, production and sale of cosmetics and related items through its own shops and franchise outlets. The company began trading in the UK in 1976 and now operates 900 stores in 41 countries. It employs in excess of 2,000 staff and has an annual turnover of over £150 million.

Success factors

The company is very successful and has grown by 131 per cent in the last five years. It has high-median industrial quartiles for return on capital and return on total assets. The company has developed its overseas operations successfully; overseas outlets now contribute 50 per cent of its turnover.

Reasons for success

The company believes its success can be attributed to a number of factors:

- company image
- innovative approach to business
- quality and cost of products
- distinctive brand
- good management

The company's image varies from country to country: in the UK, for example, the company has strong associations with societal and environmental values, whereas Americans associate the company with natural products. The company has an innovative approach to business in that it operates both a financial and an environmental bottom line.

The company's products are of good quality and are fairly priced, especially when compared with other cosmetic products. Another important success factor is the distinctive nature of its retail outlets and the distinctive look of its products; it can be described as making an unambiguous and very focused retailing and visual merchandizing effort. The fifth success factor is good management. As a franchise company, it has been very well managed, and care has been taken to keep costs under control. The company has experienced rapid organic growth which has been managed successfully.

Measures of success

The company measures its success in a number of ways. Quality of management is seen to be very useful in achieving success, although the company feels this is virtually impossible to measure. Financial soundness, product quality and the ability to innovate are all considered very important. The company takes environmental responsibility very seriously and believes this also contributes to its success.

As mentioned earlier, the company has two bottom lines. Like all businesses, the company must make money; this is the financial bottom line. The second bottom line has three components: environmental responsibility, animal protection and human rights. The company has an environmental audit that enables it to assess its impact on the environment; it has commissioned outside firms to measure variables relating to energy consumption *per capita*, waste management, the use of paper products, etc. It is in the process of introducing a social audit to measure variables relating to its social responsibility.

The company also uses standard financial measures—growth rates, margins and operating profit. It does not use traditional retail measures because it is essentially a wholesaler selling its own manufactured products to franchisees.

Competitors

The company feels it has no real direct competitors in the UK. The largest threat comes from a new entrant to the UK market, a US company that specializes in novelty bath and cosmetics products. The competition is very much country specific. For example, in the US the company has a large number of smaller rivals that produce natural cosmetic products.

The company's information systems enable it to monitor its own performance effectively, but it is not very effective at monitoring changes in market conditions generally. Monitoring competitors in the UK market is not considered particularly important.

The company monitors two additional variables: country specific demographics and government legislation. It is considered very important to monitor changes in population demographics in various countries. For example, the demography of the US is changing dramatically: at present approximately one in eight of the population is aged over 65, but at the start of the next century this figure is likely to be one in three. This will have an enormous impact on the company.

The company also monitors changes in legislation and in the legal framework of the countries it operates in. This is especially important when it comes to product ranges that are classified as pharmaceuticals in certain global markets, since the pharmaceutical industry is heavily regulated in most countries.

Information technology and information systems

As a retail company, company L has to collect and analyze sales and market information in order to remain competitive. It plans to introduce an electronic point of sale (EPOS) system in its retail outlets and this will have a fundamental impact on revenue. The company acts as wholesaler, supplying products to franchised shops, and the EPOS system will increase the efficiency of the supply chain. The company also plans to use EDI systems to speed up the supply side of the business.

User involvement

The business users are the main sponsors of the systems; the systems implementation process is carried out as a partnership between the company's IT department and the users, with the business user owning the project.

The company feels it is difficult to achieve a balance between user involvement and professional control in the systems development process. In the past IT departments have delivered systems without consulting user departments at all. Over the last couple of years the balance has swung too far the other way, and users have chosen systems without consulting IT professionals about what is possible or how they will fit in with existing systems. It is extremely important, therefore, that dialogue between the user and IT department is tightly controlled and understood on both sides.

The company is trying to introduce the EPOS system as the retailers' rather than the IT department's system, so the business users are very much involved in the development process. The system will be the retailer's tool, so the project director is a retail manager. This level of user participation is not applied to every system; both systems with a high technical component and simple desktop applications are the responsibility of the IT department.

Information technology

E-mail is used extensively for internal communications and is considered to be very effective. EDI systems are being investigated, as is the use of videoconferencing to communicate with the US-based business.

The company does not design systems in-house, and has a software package approach. Capital is allocated to information systems at board level, but this follows no formal process, with the board making judgements based on its own feelings about what systems would most benefit the company.

The company feels information systems can be split into two broad types: systems designed to improve productivity, and information management systems. The potential benefits to the business of introducing the first type of system can be tested before implementation; a business case can be made for spending capital on such a system, i.e. it will improve productivity by a factor of x. The same cannot be said about information management systems, so any decisions about spending capital on this type of system are made at a senior level, based on the feelings of senior staff.

Information strategy

The company believes that it does not require an information strategy as such, although it recognizes that information strategies can have an impact on certain types of business.

According to the company, there are different ways of defining what is meant by the term. In the past, it meant 'whether you were with IBM or not'; in other words, the specific hardware and software used to provide information systems defined the information strategy.

The company takes a different approach: the information strategy refers to decisions about the information systems required by the business, taking into account its position in the market and how it competes in that market. In this context the company's two main strategies can be described as:

- operate an open systems environment; keep all options to do with products and technologies in the future as open as possible
- use software packages; go for tried and tested software solutions, adopt a solid approach.

The company feels there are two routes to information systems development: develop systems in-house, or buy a package. The first route is considered too expensive in the long run. The second route involves two additional options. One is to define a specification and ask a software company to adapt its software to the specification—in other words, customization of the package. The second option—the one favoured by the company—is to show a software company the business requirement and ask them how their software can fulfil it. The company stated it would rather change the way it does its business than change the software that provides its information systems.

Evaluating information systems

The company has no formal methods of evaluating its information systems. It believes that the cost of computing power is so low that IT is now becoming almost a commodity. It has adopted a package approach to systems selection; if any system fails to achieve what was required it is simply replaced.

The company knowledge base

The company understands that information is of value but feels it relies more heavily on individuals' knowledge and expertise in order to remain successful. It would not call itself an information intensive company; rather, in comparison with other large retailers, it feels it places more emphasis on people than information.

Information resources

The company does have a library—a small collection of reference books to which staff have access.

Knowledge transfer

Individuals' knowledge and expertise is communicated to other members of staff verbally; knowledge transfer depends on individuals rather than on systems. It is a young company and many of the original members are still in post. The company feels it is structured around people rather than functions.

Information transfer

The company has a fairly large communications department which ensures that important items are circulated to staff automatically. This information covers both internal information and information describing the company's external activities. The company head office is designed to facilitate verbal communication, with open plan office areas. In addition, the company transfers knowledge electronically, via company television, by newsletter, and through regular 'value' meetings.

Most information is transferred via e-mail (the company is taking steps to reduce the amount of paper it uses in the business). A newsletter is circulated to all staff. The company also has its own television production facility which produces videos describing the work of the company, how well it is performing, and its external interests. The videos are circulated to company retail outlets where staff are encouraged to watch them.

Regular presentations are organized throughout the company to communicate information to staff and to allow staff to discuss issues affecting the company. These are called 'value' meetings, and are given a high priority by the board. The company believes that in general there is very little information that does not circulate freely.

Problems locating information

There are some problems locating information once it is inside the company. Typically, information relating to specific products tends may be difficult to find. Another problem is that pockets of information tend to build up in certain areas and these may be inaccessible to some staff. However, the company feels these problems are common to most organizations.

Information ethos

The company recognizes the value of information, and places a great deal of emphasis on the open exchange of information with everyone from the shop floor level upwards. It feels it has an ethos that encompasses a very proactive approach to employee communications. An important element of this is an openness on all issues. The information flows in both directions, from the company to the staff and from the staff back to the company.

Information and business objectives

The company's key business objectives are not fully defined, beyond that of operating two bottom lines—financial and socio-environmental. Actual financial objectives are not specifically defined; for example, the company does not think it is necessary to measure market share. One identifiable financial business objective is to achieve a compound growth rate of 20 per cent in terms of profits. This is a short term target; the company does not have any long term financial goals.

Essentially, the company's objectives are to remain at the forefront of business and social change, to continue to develop top quality products, to continue to innovate, and to continue to penetrate global markets effectively.

The company's information systems provide information that enables it to achieve these objectives. However, it does not attempt to align information systems with specific business objectives. Rather, information systems are seen to be necessary to do business in the 1990s—they are a minimal ticket of entry into the marketplace.

Training and human resources

The company makes considerable effort to train staff in IT and information skills. Staff are given training tokens which they can redeem at the company IT school. This system appears to work very well. The company is looking at ways of developing staff into 'super users'; that is, giving staff the skills they require to operate in the information age, rather than just IT training to do the job.

In general, the company feels staff are aware of all the information resources available to them.

SECTION 3
THE SEMINAR

Introduction

A seminar was held on 13th March 1995 at the British Library Research and Development Department in order to give the researchers an opportunity to discuss the initial findings of the investigation with selected representatives of the information profession. In the first part of the seminar the research results were presented. In the second part, three information practitioners from the corporate sector were invited to give their response. There was an open discussion of the issues raised.

Presentation of results

Overview: Professor Tom Wilson

Professor Wilson explained that the project was only part way through, and outlined its background. The project originated with a seminar held in Finland. As a result of this meeting the participants decided that, in effect, they represented a 'consortium', which should try to find funding to take forward the ideas discussed. In the event funding was only secured by the UK participants. At this meeting a framework was produced for all to work to, representing the relation between company performance and effective information systems (Figure 7). The framework shows that such systems are themselves dependent on certain factors: technology, company knowledge base, information sensitivity, and company information ethos. The framework illustrated represents a simplified form—the relationships are in fact more complex than this.

There are different ways in which this framework could be tested, and the method chosen was influenced by the funding available. It was decided to go for a qualitative exploration, a first stab at demonstrating that the model represents reality in organizations.

Figure 7

Organization structure/culture

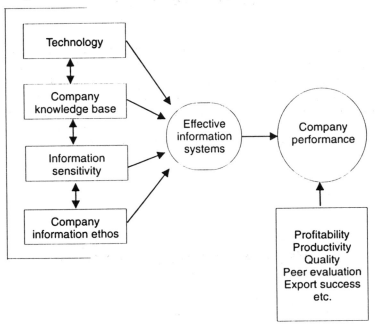

The organizations selected for the study had to fulfil certain criteria:

- be in the median or upper quartiles of their industry
- appear in the *Times 500* list
- appear in the *Euro 500* list
- appear in *Britain's Most Admired Company* study

They were all 'high performance' companies, judged according to the attributes listed in the framework: profitability, productivity, quality, peer evaluation, export success. The actual sample was chosen from within this range and represents an interesting mix of companies (the actual companies are not identified).

Within their own sectors these are all high performing companies. Their rankings by sales are as follows (some were not available or directly comparable):

Company	Position	Company	Position
Company A	1st	Company G	3rd
Company B	N/A	Company H	N/A
Company C	4th	Company I	11th
Company D	2nd	Company J	6th
Company E	N/A	Company K	21st
Company F	1st	Company L	5th

Were the companies information intensive or non-intensive? The study asked the managers concerned what they thought, and according to this the sample fell into two equal groups:

Intensive	Non-intensive
Company B	Company A
Company C	Company D
Company E	Company F
Company G	Company I
Company H	Company J
Company L	Company K

Some of those in the non-intensive group thought that this was changing and that they were becoming more information intensive, sometimes due to the influence of a new CEO bringing about cultural change in the company.

The study looked specifically at the four aspects of organizational structure/culture listed in the framework as determining effective information systems: technology, company knowledge base, information sensitivity, company information ethos.

In terms of technology, managers were asked whether their information systems were keyed to business objectives. Some believed that this was not the case. Most did seem to believe that they had effective information systems.

In terms of the company knowledge base, all believed that this was heavily dependent on individuals—individuals' knowledge of the market, etc.—and this was not effectively managed through information systems. Some companies had experienced certain restraints on introducing IT systems (e.g. need to conform to industry regulations) and information systems were suffering as a consequence of this. There was a very gloomy view of the role of libraries; where they existed they did not provide support to all business functions and made little effort to promote their activities. Over the last ten years IT divisions within organizations have been moving closer to business departments and it is now very common to have teams of IT and business partners. Perhaps special libraries have something to learn here about building relationships.

Information sensitivity was evaluated by asking participants how effectively their information systems enabled the company to monitor three key areas: their own performance, the performance of their main competitors, and changes in the market in general. Information systems were not seen as very effective in these three areas. The problem seems to lie in those areas where special libraries could play a role—if the necessary relationships have been built up. However, there is a recognition that information systems are not making external information available.

To judge the information ethos of the companies, participants were asked what efforts the company made towards training in IT and information skills. In most companies some, and in several companies, considerable, effort was made in this area. However, it was almost exclusively concerned with *internal* systems. A second question asked participants how effectively the company's attitude towards information ensured that the value of information was conveyed to all workers. There was a much wider spread here, with the largest group sitting firmly on the fence. There was also a difference in the answers elicited by interview and those by questionnaire: answers given in interviews were rather more non-committal.

Conclusions

- All companies showed wide experience in IT solutions for information systems (IS).
- Successful IS have been developed with the IS department working in close partnership with business functions. What is the role of special libraries in this? There was very little evidence of effective working with business functions—their approach was responsive rather than proactive.
- The majority of companies have a formal IS planning process. However, there was little in the way of formalized information service development plans.
- The more successful companies have benefited from top management commitment to IT and information in general.
- Companies have emphasized the importance of balance between involvement of user departments and technical IS or IT functions in the design of information systems.
- However, in the thrust towards IT all effort has been in that direction and not towards the development of information services.
- All company libraries have seen their staff and funding diminish and they have been slow to take up new technology. There has been increasing marginalization of library-based services in favour of technology-based services, which lack the expertise of libraries.
- Commitment from the top is essential. IS development in the more successful companies has been led by the CEO.
- Senior staff are more concerned with presentation and speed than with the quality of the information they receive.
- They also pay more attention to internal information than to information about the market and competitors.
- User training in IT and information skills has emerged as an important factor in the successful implementation of IS.
- All companies have mechanisms for circulating information around the company. However, these mechanisms concentrate on horizontal rather than vertical information transfer. In other

words, significant areas of information do not get through to the right people.

What of the framework which provided the starting point of the study? The study concluded that the framework does exist in reality, but that other factors are also significant. These are:

- The attitude of the CEO—if involved and committed, it works.
- Internal politics. Without a focused vision, internal politics play a bigger role, leading to 'turbulence', which inhibits effective information systems.
- The state of the market. This plays a part in determining how much money is available for development.
- The nature of the industry itself—what constitutes competitive advantage.
- Changes in the nature of competition, e.g. privatization, entry of new and bigger players.
- Changes in legislation and government regulation, which can have an impact on the urgency and need to develop information services.

The project could now be taken a stage further, using the standardized instruments developed during the study.

Two case studies: Ian Owens

The interview and questionnaire schedule was based on the premises of the framework, as shown above in Figure 7. For the purposes of this seminar, two case studies were chosen, one at each end of the scale:

- Company A was a very large water provider, with some overseas operations. Total sales: 1,093,200 (£000s). Number of employees: 10,141.
- Company F had the majority of its operations overseas, especially the Pacific rim, but in the UK was badly hit by the recession and was on the verge of failing. Total sales: 2,737,400 (£000s). Number of employees: 41,100.

In the area of technology, company A emphasized the CEO's role in the effective development and implementation of IT. In company F all decisions regarding technology were made at corporate level; users identified needs and then put these to the corporate decision-makers. There was a perceived need to harmonize use of technology across departments; in taking over other businesses they had inherited a variety of systems.

Looking at the company knowledge base, in company A the library acted more as a repository of information, with information provided on demand. A lack of resources meant that it was unable actively to promote services. In company F information was provided on an 'as needs' basis. The impression given was of a scattergun approach to information; because people had no idea where it came from or who had provided it, it was difficult to determine its value.

The information sensitivity questions also revealed different attitudes. Information circulated in company A appeared to focus on key facts and comparative indicators: a collection of cuttings was compiled along with relevant information about regulation, etc., and circulated electronically via floppy disc. In company F, in contrast, some information was gathered from external sources, but it was difficult for users to identify where.

In terms of information ethos, there were again very different results. Company A had instituted 'Project Breakthrough', an ongoing project developed over five years, designed to win hearts and minds and based on needs, which aims to create a culture and environment for the successful implementation of information systems; this is now beginning to show benefits. In company F information was disseminated on a need-to-know basis, with the result that information was held at too high a level, and managers were unsure how much to pass on down the line.

Conclusions

- Company A has a culture that enables effective information systems development and sees this culture as providing a major competitive advantage.
- The very different ethos in company F, on the other hand, has restricted the development of effective information systems and they do not see the necessity for information dissemination.
- In company A the CEO has provided a framework for effective information systems; this is not apparent in F.

Implications for the information profession:
Angela Abell

Angela Abell explained that her comments would be based partly on the findings of this study, but also on other work and projects carried out. These included:

- The initial feasibility study for the current project, funded by BLRDD. This involved, firstly, a literature review to find out what work had been done on information culture and its effect on performance. Much has been written about organizational culture; where the culture is more adaptive and places emphasis on the individual, companies tend to be more successful. Another finding of the review was that successful introduction of IT depended on effective leadership from the top. The second part of the study involved case studies based on a questionnaire survey. All participants felt that their organizations were information-based. All viewed information as something they relied on—but all had very different ideas of what information meant. What they had in common was that they wanted information keyed into real, practical problems.
- A DTI-funded study on information use by SMEs. This took a specific problem in each SME and looked at whether electronic information sources could help solve them. It found that electronic information sources were not much help in solving these specific problems.
- Study of information use by European biotechnology and robotics industries, funded by the European Commission.
- The RSA inquiry into *Tomorrow's Company* (published in July 1995). This has looked at the structure of companies and applied different measures of success to them. All came back to the people involved and how individuals work. Information appears to be an invisible asset, which companies are not organized to exploit.
- Discussions with consultancy clients and practitioners.

All the evidence appears to indicate that information is moving more towards the centre of concern within organizations. Good information management is central to:

- empowerment
- the learning organization
- benchmarking approaches to management
- flatter organizational structures

There is now interest in company knowledge as an intangible 'balance sheet' asset, together with the realization that knowledge systems should integrate operational data, company intelligence and external information.

This interest forms part of current thinking in management practices, but it is also a function of 'IT pull'. However, there has been a shift in focus from dependence on the IT department to an approach driven by user requirements. This includes a change:

- from operational, financial and design software to groupware and communications
- from creation of databases to document management, workflow, imaging.

Users are becoming much more involved in the design of information delivery systems through the need to share information and experience. At the same time, many organizations are now developing IT strategies; this may be a fashion, but it is helping to bring about more effective use of IT systems. Users' perceptions are changing as:

- information suppliers target end users and begin to provide attractive and relevant products
- IT suppliers improve software, hardware, systems, communications and application sharing for the individual
- media attention makes IT seem part of life
- the growth of the Internet brings IT and information into everyday life.

The acquisition of information is focused on 'real-time' as the Internet and Microsoft hold out the 'real-time promise' to everyone.

Whatever the impetus, within organizations the IT focus is changing to an Information Systems focus and sometimes to an Information Utilization focus, encompassing both internal and external information.

Alongside users' perceptions, attitudes to information are also undergoing change. The issues here for the information professional are:

- who is implementing the outcomes of this change?
- who is designing the information systems and flows?
- what impact is the information profession having as a whole?
- how are special libraries influencing the developments?
- does the profession concentrate too much on 'our point of view', rather than note what is really happening?

It appears that the real innovation and developments are being driven by other people within the organization—once the IT department, then the IS department, and now managers of business process or functional departments.

In this changing environment, what skills are needed? Core information skills are crucial to the successful design and implementation of systems, but there is no guarantee that the information profession will be the source for these. As other disciplines implement IS systems they will acquire the necessary information retrieval skills themselves. What new skills are needed for corporate information units to become key players in the new information based organizations?

- political ability
- business acumen
- personnel skills
- in-depth IT skills
- management and communication skills
- ability to innovate and negotiate
- ability to become part of the organization
- well-developed project management skills

Information managers often have the ideas, but lack the ability to push them through—this is left to others who have more political ability and real understanding of how the business works. We are working with people who understand their business, but the information profession is from *outside*, and so has to learn it.

To what extent does the influence of the corporate library or information unit depend on where it fits into the organizational structure and who funds it? Traditionally they were part of R&D or marketing departments. Then there was a move to an 'office management' approach with, in some cases, the information function expanding to control functions such as records and archives management, word processing, communications, etc. In some institutions there has been some integration with IT, but this convergence is largely confined to the academic sector. The aim in the corporate sector is to see 'Information on the Board'—Director level information posts within organizations, but these are rare. However, successful information systems need Chief Executive backing. This suggests that the information profession will have to acquire the skills to influence those who operate at Board level.

One of the main barriers to achieving such influence is the perceived 'place' of the information professional within the firm and its industry. Too often the library or information unit is viewed as the 'bubble on the side', as a support unit, not as part of the organization. Bankers in banking, engineers in engineering, are an integral part of their business and industry. On the other hand, support staff bring specialist skills, but these are not perceived as necessarily industry specific. There are exceptions, but generally the corporate information professional is not viewed as, and finds it difficult to feel, 'part of the business'.

Support functions are vulnerable to contracting out. There is some evidence to suggest that this may be happening to parts of the process—acquisition, distribution, organization of materials—but the control of information systems such as EIS is seen as too important. These are being undertaken by other parts of the organization and are more likely to be designed by end users. In other words, the easy things are contracted out, while the difficult parts remain in-house. *Information* is seen as core, but the information *profession* is not.

How do we integrate the information profession into the corporate world? The accountancy and law professions have achieved this through exploitation of legal requirement. While there may be some parallels with copyright and disclosure regulation, the information profession needs to understand the true potential of its role.

What are the implications for the profession?

- *Education—primary/secondary sectors.* What is the role of the professional in educating children/students in information use?
- *Education of the information profession.* What type of education is needed? What should we be teaching? When is the best time? Is there a place for specialist library education?
- *A new profession.* Is the information profession redundant (an old question)? How do we go about attracting the high flyers into the profession? How does it become integrated into the life of its corporate sponsors?

- *Reliable and relevant information delivery.* Is there a role in evaluating the quality of information supplied to users? How can information professionals acquire sufficient understanding of their organizations/industries? Should they concentrate on facilitating appropriate access and delivery mechanisms? Should their focus be on the development of new information services?
- *The information industry.* Explode or implode? There are two possible ways of looking at the future. One sees a huge potential market with new end users. The other sees a declining market, which has become too narrow and restricted by internal information systems.
- *The future.* Who will be the change agents in the information world — the profession? — the suppliers? — or the emerging breed of innovative users?

Discussion

In the two case studies, Company A (water business) was involved with one product. What was the product mix in F?

The primary products are glass and building materials. Different products were involved, and also different production activities. Company F has a global production process. In terms of information systems, the nature of the industry does have an impact.

In the case of A, what was the impact of moving from the public to private sector?

There was a desire to move away from the public sector association and practices. An example of this is the changes introduced in the handling of customer complaints; these formerly went to one department and there was no flow of information through the company.

There has been a flow of information professionals into the water companies. Was there any evidence of an inheritance in continuing use of information?

It was hard to tell if the legacy still exists. It may have helped to engender the sense that information is significant and therefore made the organization more receptive to a new CEO determined to change the culture.

Both A and F were classed as information non-intensive. Was this deliberate in their selection as case studies?
It was more important that they were at either end of the scale. All the others fall in between.

In the interview survey, were companies prompted as to whether they were information intensive or non-intensive?
It was thought of as a difficult area and so the interviewers had prompts ready. However, they were not necessary as the participants jumped at the question—they had been thinking about this area. There is an increasing awareness of information. In SMEs, however, there would be a different response. Some companies say that they are totally reliant on information—but by 'information' they mean something different from the profession's view of it.

Does the question of information intensive / non-intensive relate to internal or external information?
This is not as clear cut as it might seem. It involves monitoring external information as well as intensive use of internal information. Market information is vital. Successful people have a different way of keeping their finger on the pulse. It is to do with using information as *intelligence*—intelligence drives the company. The information profession must tackle the problem of turning information into intelligence, if it is to be useful. This is brain-intensive activity, and it is in conflict with the view of IT as dispensing with individual input—systems which are developed to handle information in a person-detached fashion.

If the library/information unit remains the 'bubble on the side' and is not integrated, it will find it very difficult to provide intelligence to the company.
The fault is spread across all the players. As a profession we have not tried to make an impact through the right channels. For instance, reviews of successful practice may be found in the LIS literature, but nothing appears in, for example, *Management Today* or the *Financial Times*. Effort needs to be focused here if we are to persuade companies of the importance of intelligence.

We are thinking of intelligence as a 'hand-made' thing. Should we moving towards a 'factory-made' view—now made possible by new technology?

The PR section traditionally carried out this key function of intelligence. The diffusion of the intelligence role though the organization is probably inevitable. The role of the information profession is to manage and distribute it.

Did the survey address the question of information overload?
In the two case studies information overload was not seen as a particular problem. Other companies in the survey did feel they were overwhelmed. The scattergun approach to information was quite common. One highly valued role of the information profession is in selecting and filtering—putting on the manager's desk exactly the information required.

What is the connection between problem recognition and the information department? Intelligence is asking the right questions, not giving the right answers. There is a difference between the concept of the problem and finding the solution—the latter is not the interesting part.
Those with wide experience know exactly where and who to go to for solutions to problems—but none said they would go to the information department or library for them.

Responses to the research findings

First response: Melanie Goody, KPMG Peat Marwick

It would have been interesting to have had a comparison of two organizations—one performing well and one badly—in the *same* sector. It is difficult to judge how much meaningful information can be gained from a comparison of companies in different sectors. A key element in the success of company A was the CEO; the drivers for change are the people at Board level. It would be interesting to investigate the role of the information professional in these successful organizations.

One comment from the survey was particularly horrifying—'we haven't got the resources to promote the library'. In the profession we tend to assume that people should realize how good libraries are. Instead, we have to make a very good business case for libraries.

The companies investigated seemed to lack cooperation between the information and IT departments. This seems a strange division, since many information professionals would be unable to do their jobs without the support of the IT department. IT people tend to take the view that information and technology are different and separate, but they are quite willing to cooperate because they are not risking their own empire. Together they provide a better service than with each working individually. In contrast, there is often a defensive reaction from the traditional information professional who fears the loss of his/her job.

'Information' can be seen as having three stages:

- Data
- Information
- Knowledge, which is information interpreted and applied.

Increasingly, data now go straight to the end user, and we risk the loss of stage two. Users often do not know where information is coming from, making it very difficult to interpret or evaluate. This is where the information profession must promote its role in this process—in interpretation and evaluation. Everyone is becoming more IT literate; we should help in the process of making users more *information* literate. We should be going out from the library to make sure that people have access to the information they want, rather than waiting for them to come to us.

Second response: Graham Hickley, BBC

The study confirms our worst fears and prejudices. Abroad, the impression of British management and use of IT is that we are way behind. It was interesting to have this confirmed—but they also think that the rest of Europe is even further behind.

The knowledge base is still heavily dependent on individuals. There is still a strong tendency to hold information at the highest level and exchange it through interpersonal contact, rather than through a systematic approach—the 'old boy network' is still there. It is difficult to approach senior members of corporations because we don't speak the same language. Information professionals are not good at selling themselves—but they must do this in order to break through the 'glass ceiling'. Some companies in the study blamed the sensitivity of staff members as having prevented the introduction of IT developments for information systems. This is not good enough—it is just an excuse for doing nothing. The information profession tends to be nervous of IT and changes in work; they see it as a long term threat to their jobs.

In talking of the 'information profession', we are in danger of creating a little ghetto. We should be thinking more in terms of the information manager with training in information. The job could easily be done by someone without formal information qualifications. We risk painting ourselves into a corner; the 'bubble on the side' will fall off because others will take our role—PR and IT have already been mentioned. It is important that we do not consider ourselves as separate.

Information is fundamental to the business process. It is ubiquitous. We try to pull out one bit to call our own, but this is only one part of the mix of internal and external information needed for the decision-making process. This is why people worry about promoting the library. In ten years time commercial libraries will be providing information, not library services, and companies with traditional libraries will go bust.

There is always plenty of money for information services, provided that it is seen as a clear business requirement; it must make money for the rest of the corporation and benefit the business as a whole. It should not be difficult to demonstrate this. We should be looking to expand our empires, to take in the IT and PR functions, for example. However, no money will be forthcoming if all you want is to be a library.

Third response: Mark Jewel, Lehmen Brothers

The last point about money is very important. We must present the case for the library as a business case. Librarians have problems dealing with this perception. In the financial services sector, managing the corporate library is only a very small part of the information manager's job; the library unit is a business unit within the corporation. We must change perceptions: our affinities should not be with the profession, or with the library, but with the corporation and its business objectives.

The amount of information available has changed radically; the annual reports in banking are an example. Libraries in the banking sector have seen a change in personnel; there is now a different sort of person in post to deal with these new resources. The way we perceive our roles is crucially important—as a 'bubble on the side' we will certainly drop off.

Information will become much more of a commodity product, with emphasis on standardization and the ease with which it can be obtained. Information is not as important as intelligence. The key role of the information professional is to work with the IT department to package information for clients and end users. To do this we have to be able to understand the client's business—and this involves getting close to the client. Traditional library work will become rarer because, as a hand-delivered product, it will be too expensive.

What is the future for librarians? They will be business people first, with information skills grafted on. They will understand IT skills (rather than taking a hands-on or 'screwdriver' approach to IT). They will do other things within the organization as well. As information managers, their role will incorporate other activities. They will end up with a cohesive area of expertise which is required by their business sector. They will be part of the back room support for the organization, with responsibility for non-real time information services. All this has significant implications for the education of librarians.

Summary of responses: Professor Tom Wilson

Professor Wilson summed up the responses and discussion thus far:

- The information culture or role of the CEO represents the key to success.
- There is a fuzzy area between the IT and the information service. Should this grow even fuzzier?
- Making a clear business case is the key to any development in information services.
- The reluctance of British management generally to take hold of the role of IT in organizations may relate to their view of information services in the organization.
- The situation found in the case studies does not hold true for the financial services sector, perhaps because it is more advanced than the manufacturing sector.

In the light of these points, the strategy for developing effective information systems would appear to involve three key actions:

- Forge a strategic alliance with IT
- Develop proactive services and forge links with the business
- Find, or become, a champion to convince the CEO of the value of information services.

Discussion

Some of these concepts were around twenty-five years ago. It is fundamental to show that you are helping the business to go forward—why do we have to keep reminding ourselves of this?

The study shows that many are not aware of these fundamental concepts. The problem is how to get through to the people who do not see the need to demonstrate effectiveness.

In the successful companies, is there a strong management culture? Perhaps we should be looking at this rather than at information in isolation. High performing companies will always get more use out of information: could this have skewed the results?

We recognized this in the study, but decided on high performing companies as a starting point. At the other end of the scale the situation could be disastrous. The study aimed to look at information systems within the organizational context.

Does it come down to education? New entrants make the same mistakes and go through the same process. We are not getting through at that level.

The LIS Department at Sheffield University regularly carries out follow-up studies of its students. These have generally found that, up to the third job, they always stress the technical aspects (now IT) of the course as the most useful. Thereafter management ideas are uppermost. As they proceed up the ladder they generally realize that they need to be better equipped for the management role. An information management option within the MBA at Sheffield was so successful that they had to cut it because they were losing numbers on the rest of the course. All the graduates went on to interesting jobs—key information roles in business management, but not traditional information roles. Different people are being attracted into these new roles, and at the same time the information function is becoming more diffuse across the organization rather than isolated in special units. A shift is taking place, but it is a slow, gradual process. The effects of the use of networks are moving much more quickly than the social changes. In ten years' time the problem may have disappeared naturally.

Is there any correlation between such MBA students and information aware companies? This cadre is very important to enhancing the value of information. These people are the 'champions' who can make a case for information at the highest level.

Research shows that those who have done the MBA are better equipped to seek information outside the organization. However, there is a much lower proportion of MBAs in British management than elsewhere. There is an important educational issue in preparing managers to be information aware.

We should be aiming at a multi-professional role: packaging information, adding value and presenting information in the format that people want. In the information profession we are quite good at preserving our own terrain and holding information close. Rather, the business goals of information should be paramount. Information professionals should see themselves as capable of reaching Board level, rather than moving on to the same role in another organization.

Perhaps it should be the other way round—the information professionals who take the MBA?

The problem with champions is that they may leave. If you need a champion, it betrays a lack of confidence.

Very few librarians have political ability. Perhaps this is something we should teach at library school?

Negotiation skills are taught as part of the MBA course. There are now a number of integrated courses available, e.g. business studies, financial management or accountancy offered with information management. The students on such courses see themselves as going on to business jobs. It will be interesting to track their progress to see how different their careers are from those of single honours graduates. Information management and information technology modules are now more common. This implies a greater awareness of information at entrance level, so that in twenty years' time the problem may no longer apply.

It is also important to educate from within the organization, not just at the start of careers. However, there is little development training available.

People lose jobs because they cannot develop further. The ethos of librarians sometimes works counter to what managers are trying to achieve, and there are many people around who are dragging their feet. It is not possible to accommodate everyone—some will have to move on to other types of jobs.

We are still stuck on the idea of the collection base—what the profession 'owns'. Perceptions must move away from owning to managing.

The concept of the 'crew chief' is relevant here. This developed in the US in the 1940s. The essential idea is that the crew owns the aircraft and allows the pilot to fly it; the most important thing for everyone is the success of the mission. If we regard information as the mission, our role becomes one of maintenance, to ensure that the mission does not fail. If you give people a mission, it may generate a different perception. In other words, we should give people ownership of and responsibility for what they do.

Another way to achieve this is to give people a mission to serve different groups, with the aim of not getting any complaints. At the same time they should be encouraged to spend time outside the library, to go and seek out their customers. This is difficult because people will say they haven't the time—they have 'work to do'. In reference libraries, work 'on the counter' is not seen as real work.

This is essentially the same concept—they are both mission oriented.

The solutions to the problems lie in education. No one is born a manager—it has to be learned. Library schools should follow this example. Management culture has to be taught. This is as important as teaching business students the importance of information. If business people are informed about the value of information and its use and handling, it makes our job easier: they will be more prepared to seek and take advice from information professionals.

Information professionals are much better at talking to each other than at communicating with others. We will not achieve these changes until we are more effective at communicating outside the profession. Media interest and use of the Internet have raised awareness of informa-tion—not the information profession.

We must also be able to deliver. If we publish outside the professional press, we must be able to deliver what we promise; this doesn't always happen.

Perhaps we should be targeting the real audience, rather than the insulated profession. A good example of this was some research carried out at Sheffield University which was aimed at Social Services Depart-ments. One member of the research team had journalistic flair, with the result that the project was much more widely covered in the social sciences literature than in the information literature. It produced a measurable effect, with the research much more widely cited than is usually the case.

There are signs of long term change in the profession. The primary role will be one of managing and evaluating systems and products. There will also be fewer of us.

There is likely to be more of us scattered through the organization, rather than in information units. There was a similar effect in cataloguing departments when computer based catalogues arrived; those displaced found other information roles in the system. There may be a reduction in central services staff, but this will be balanced by an expansion of numbers within the organization.

Another element in this picture will be contracting out. However it is achieved, the aim is still to get the mission accomplished.

The custom work may be what is contracted out. It will be the information manager's role to manage this distribution to get the job done.

What about the role of 'information gatekeepers'? Do they still exist?

They do still exist, often as a particular personality type. The term has vanished from the information literature, but has reappeared in other sectors, sometimes under a different name.

People are now expected take in information and react to it very quickly. This has led to an increased use of e-mail and abstract information, rather than the original documentation. If people are using abstracts as the source, this raises the question of the quality of abstracting. We are responsible for the quality of the information we provide.

This is one of the key skills—discriminating between good and bad sources.

Another problem linked to the last point is that the knowledge/experience base is not being maintained in organizations. The pressure is for instantaneous delivery; taking stock is regarded as time-wasting. One of our roles must be to operate against this trend, to sustain the 'corporate memory'.

What makes a corporate department successful? It would be very useful to be able to isolate those factors which contribute to success. These would also have important implications for education.

Different skills are required at different stages and levels of the development of the company. We need both those who initiate change and those who come in behind to do the maintenance.

Are our problems embedded in national approaches? It would be most interesting to carry this project further to other countries and to carry out comparisons of approach. And this should go further than Europe; Australians, for example, have a tradition of 'go and see'—going to see for themselves other ways of doing things—but British business doesn't believe in this.

APPENDICES

Appendix 1: The Interview Schedule

<u>Cover Sheet</u>

Name:
Company:
Department:
Position:

Date:
Interview Start Time:
Interview Stop Time:
Total Duration:

<u>Interview Constraints</u>

Section 1. **Success Factors.**

To begin with I would like to ask some questions about the success of your company, the measures you use to identify success and how far company success depends on effective information.

1. Firstly, in general how successful do you feel the company is, in relation to the industry as a whole?

Response:

2. What would you say are the main reasons for the company's success [*or lack of success*] in the industry?

Response:

3. How would you rate the following as effective measures of success?[**probe**: *show R response card 1*]

Response:

4. Does your company use any other measures of success?

No   Yes

4.1. What are they?[**probe**: *ask R to note them on response card 2*]

Response:

4.2. How would you rate its/their usefulness on the same scale?[**probe**: *use response card 2*]

Response:

5. Do you have many competitors?

No   Yes

5.1. Can you please name your main competitor.

....

5.2 How would you rate your main competitor on the same success criteria. [**probe**: *show R response card 3*]

Response:

6. Can you tell me how far the company's information systems enable it to monitor aspects of the market on this card? [**probe**: *show R response card 4*]

Response:

7. Are there any other aspects of company performance that you believe it is necessary to monitor? [**probe**: *show R response card 5*]

No   Yes

7.1. How effectively is this done by your company? [**probe:** *note answer on response card 5*]

Response:

Section 2. **Information Technology & Information Systems**

In this section I would like you to tell me how information technology is used as a delivery tool for information systems and information services, covering both internal and external information.

8. Can you tell me how far users of information systems are involved in the design of these systems? [**prompt**: *user surveys. user participation in planning meetings.....*]

Response:

9. Can you tell me if the company uses any of the following IT applications in the provision of information systems or information services?

No   Yes

9.1. Please indicate how effective you think they are.[**probe**: *give R response card 6*]

Response:

10. Please describe how the company identified and decided which IT applications were used and developed for the provision of information systems? [**prompt:** *please elaborate..*]

Response:

11. Can you identify an information systems strategy in the company?[**prompt:** *Do information systems figure in the company's strategic planning process*]

No   Yes

11.1. What are the key elements of this strategy?

Response:

12. Do you evaluate the effectiveness of your information systems?

No   Yes

12.1 How often, and please describe the evaluation process?

Response:

13. In general, in what ways do you think your information systems and services affect the long term effectiveness/competitiveness of the company in relation to other industrial participants?[**prompt**: *Please elaborate*]

Response:

Section 3. The Company Knowledge Base.

In this section I will be asking you questions about what constitutes the company's knowledge base, and how far the knowledge base is at risk through dependency on individuals rather than systems.

14. Does the company have any library facilities, or information centres where information is stored?

No   Yes

14.1. Are different types of information kept separately?

[**prompt**: *please explain*]

Response:

15. Does your company require a great deal of information to remain competitive, or does success depend on individual's knowledge and expertise?

information intensive ☐

knowledge intensive ☐

15.1. Please explain your reply.

Response:

16. How is the expert knowledge of individuals within the company communicated to other members of staff [**prompt**: please elaborate..]

Response:

17. Is information automatically circulated to departments within the company?

No   Yes

17.1. What form(s) does this take for:

a) Internal information,

b) External Information

Response: a) Internal Information
b) External information

18. Do you encounter any problems locating information once it is inside the company?

No   Yes   [**prompt**: *please describe any typical problems*]

Response:

19. Please look at this list [**probe**: *hand R response card 7*] and tell me where you would go for the various types of information. and indicate how easy/difficult it is to obtain this information

Response:

Section 4. **Information Ethos**

In this final section I would like to explore how the company's attitude towards information encourages the value of information to be conveyed to all workers.

20. In general, can you describe how the company's attitude towards information ensures that the value of information is conveyed to all workers. [**prompt:** *please elaborate*]

Response:

21. What are your company's key business objectives?

Response:

```
┌─────────────────────────────────────────────────────┐
│                                                     │
└─────────────────────────────────────────────────────┘
```

22. In what ways are your information systems and services designed to achieve these objectives?

Response:

23. What efforts does the company make towards training all staff members IT and information skills?

Would you say:

- Considerable Effort ☐

- Some Effort ☐

- Little Effort ☐

- No Effort ☐

23.1. Why is that?

Response:

_____
| |
| |
| |
| |
|_____|

24. Does the company provide any additional facilities to aid staff development?
[**prompt**: *for example open-learning facilities (laser-disks), PC tutorials etc....*]

No   Yes

        24.1.   What are they?

Response:

And now the last question

25. In general, do you think staff members are aware of all the information resources that are available to them? [**prompt:** *how is this information communicated? i.e. staff meetings etc..*]

Response:

Thank you for taking part in this project.

Appendix 2: The Questionnaire

 U N I V E R S I T Y   O F   S H E F F I E L D
DEPARTMENT OF INFORMATION STUDIES
Postal address: Western Bank, Sheffield S10 2TN
Location: Regent Court, 211 Portobello Street, Sheffield S1 4DP
Tel. 0742-768555 Extns. 5080 & 5090 **Fax.** 0742-780300
Direct Line. 0742-825095

Information and Business Performance Questionnaire.

I am conducting a research project investigating the relationship between the business performance of companies and a number of information-related variables, that have been identified in earlier studies. This project is funded by the BLRDD, with as project head Professor Tom Wilson, and Ms Angela Abell, Head of Consultancy & Research at TFPL Ltd, as consultant to the study.

Following the initial stage of this investigation your organisation has been selected for inclusion in this study. The aim of this initial selection procedure was to identify those companies that could be described as 'high performing', according to a series of selection criteria.

I would like you to participate in the next stage of this investigation. This will involve completing this short questionnaire, and returning it to me **Ian Owens, Research Associate, Department of Information Studies, University of Sheffield, Western Bank, Sheffield S10 2TN** in the envelope provided as soon as possible. I would like to thank you for taking part in this project, if you require any further information please contact me at the address printed above.

Section 1: **Personal Details**

1. Name of Organisation: ....

2. Name of Department: ....

3. Position Held: ....

4. Number of years in present position:..

5. Number of years in organisation:..

Section 2: **Success Factors.**

6. How successful/unsuccessful do you feel the company is in relation to the industry as a whole? [*please tick the appropriate response box*]

Very Successful	Successful	Neutral	Not very Successful	Not at all Successful

7. What would you say are the main reasons for the company's success [or lack of success] in the industry?

Response:

8. How would you rate the following as effective measures of success?
[*please tick the appropriate response box*]

	Very useful	Useful	Neutral	Not very useful	Not at all useful
Quality of management					
Financial soundness					
Quality of products & services					
Capacity to innovate					
Strategic thinking					
Export success					
Environmental responsibility					

9. Does your company use any other measures of success?

No   Yes

    9.1 Please list any other measures of success used by your company, and then rate them on the scales provided.

    [*please write your response in the space provided, then mark your response by placing a tick in the appropriate box*]

[*response*]	Very useful	Useful	Neutral	Not very useful	Not at all useful
....					
....					
....					
....					
....					
....					
....					

10. Do you have many competitors?

No   Yes

    10.1. Please name your main competitor.

         ....

    10.2. How would you rate your main competitor on the same success criteria?

[*please mark your response by placing a tick in the appropriate box*]

	Very good	Good	Neutral	Not very good	Not at all good
Quality of management					
Financial soundness					
Quality of products & services					
Capacity to innovate					
Strategic thinking					
Export success					
Environmental responsibility					

11. How effectively do you feel the company's information systems enable it to monitor the aspects of the market printed below?

The company's information systems enable it to:
[please mark your response by placing a tick in the appropriate box]

	Very effectively	Effectively	Neutral	Not very effectively	Not at all effectively
monitor its own performance					
monitor the performance of its main competitors					
monitor changes in market conditions generally					

12. Are there any other aspects of company performance that you believe it is necessary to monitor?

No   Yes
          12.1 How effectively is this done by your company?

[please write your response in the space provided, and mark it by placing a tick in the appropriate box]

[response]	Very effectively	Effectively	Neutral	Not very effectively	Not at all effectively
....					
....					
....					
....					
....					

Section 3: **Information Technology & Information Systems**.

13. Do you use the company's information systems in your work?

No **[If no, go to section 4]**   Yes

          11.1 To what extent are you involved in the planning of these systems?

To a great degree	To some degree	Neutral	Not really	Not at all

14. Can you identify an information systems strategy in the company?

No   Yes

    14.1. What are the key elements of this strategy?

response:

15. Please indicate if you use any of the following IT applications, and indicate how effective you think they are.

[please mark your response by placing a tick in the appropriate box]

	Very effective	Effective	Neutral	Not very effective	Not at all effective
Expert systems					
Executive information systems					
E-mail					
Automatic ordering/ supply systems					
Electronic data interchange					
Voice recognition systems					
Video- conferencing/ video- transmission					

16. How far do you think your information systems and services affect the long term effectiveness/competitiveness of the company in relation to other industrial participants?

To a great degree	To some degree	Neutral	Not really	Not at all

Section 4: **The Company Knowledge Base**.

17. Does the company have any library facilities, or information centres where information is stored?
No   Yes

    17.1. Are different types of information kept separately?
    No   Yes

        17.2. Please describe these facilities.

response
:

18. Does your company require a great deal of information to remain competitive, or does success depend on individual's knowledge and expertise?[*please circle the appropriate response*]

a) Information   b) Knowledge

19. How is the expert knowledge of individuals within the company communicated to other members of staff?

response:

20. Is any information automatically circulated to departments within the company?

No   Yes

    21.1. What form(s) does this take for:
           a) Internal information.
           b) External Information.

response:
a) Internal Information.

b) External Information.

22. Do you encounter any problems locating information once it is inside the company?

No   Yes
    22.1. Please describe any typical problems.

response:

23. Where you would go for the following information, and indicate how easy/difficult it is to obtain this information.
[*please mark your response by placing a tick in the appropriate box*]

	location/ contact	Very easy	Easy	Neutral	Difficult	Very difficult
Technical Information						
Production Information						
Market Information						
Regulations Legislation						
Export Information						

Section 5: **Information Ethos.**

24. How do you think the company's attitude towards information ensures the value of information is effectively conveyed to all workers?

Very effectively	Effectively	Neutral	Not very effectively	Not at all effectively

25. What are your company's key business objectives?

response:

26. How effectively are your information systems and services designed to achieve these objectives?

Very effectively	Effectively	Neutral	Not very effectively	Not at all effectively

27. What efforts does the company make towards training all staff members IT and information skills?

> *Would you say:*

- Considerable Effort ☐

- Some Effort ☐

☐ Little Effort

- No Effort ☐

28. Does the company provide any facilities to aid staff development [*for example: open-learning facilities (laser disks), PC tutorials, training centres* ......]

No   Yes

> 28.1. What are they, and how often do you use them?

> *response:*

29. In general, do you think staff members are aware of all the information resources available to them?

No   Yes

> 29.1. How is this information communicated to them? [*i.e. staff meetings, company newsletter, training* ....]

> *response:*

30. Please note down any additional comments you may like to make about this questionnaire.

response:

Thank you for completing this questionnaire, all responses will be treated in confidence. Please remember to return the questionnaire as soon as psossible, to me:

Ian Owens, Research Associate, Department of Information Studies, University of Sheffield, Sheffield S10 2TN.

Thank you again for your co-operation.

Index

Page-numbers in **bold type** denote major references.